"In 'It's Lonely
Charity Maness
presenting PFC Ji
all-too-early dea
character and tru

Chronologically juxtaposing the personal and tender letters nineteen-year-old Jim wrote to his young bride, Micki, with the public facts of the war on each of those same dates, Maness artfully lets the materials speak for themselves. And they <u>do</u>--powerfully. You won't be able to put it down.

Michelle Piper's courageous move to entrust these letters to Charity Maness' care is abundantly rewarded. The author has created a heartfelt and insightful tribute to Jim Piper, the hopeful and loving young husband, and the resolute soldier he must become. What an achievement!"

Judy Hewett, MFA, Professor of English

"poignant, intimate and incredibly heart-rending"
Randy Bresee, Vietnam Era Vet '71

"powerful…compelling…"
Judy Hewett, MFA, Professor of English

"couldn't put it down"
Al Gilbert, Vietnam Veteran '66-'67

"absolute masterpiece"
Kyran Enzi, Magazine Editor

"Jim's brief life and his love for Micki, his family and his country has been thrust far beyond the granite etching on the wall in DC…"
Gary Piper, James Piper's younger brother

"It's Lonely Here in Hell"

Love Letters from Nam

By, Charity L. Maness

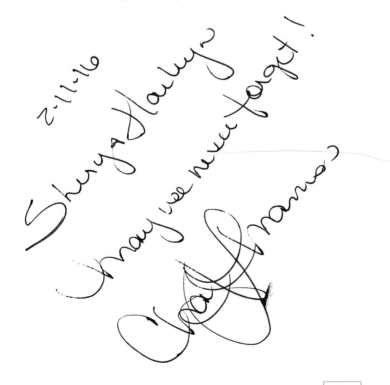

This book is dedicated to the memory of
PFC James Dennis Piper

April 28 1947

to

April 11 1967

Preface

In 2010 Michelle (Micki) Phillips, previously Michelle Piper, approached me and asked if I would be interested in writing a story based on love letters from the Vietnam War era. While my writing at the time leaned toward romance novels and cub reporting my interest was piqued. When she informed me the letters she was referring to were letters written to her from her husband who died from small arms fire in the Vietnam War leaving her a young widow, my heart broke.

On April 4, 2011, almost 44 years to the date of Jim's passing, Micki handed me a battered shoe box filled with all of Jim's handwritten letters, from his first day at boot camp to his last day in the jungles of Vietnam. I was holding history in my hands.

To be allowed the intimate glimpse into her life, the life she shared so briefly with her young husband, and to then share his letters with the world was without a doubt an honor I would not take lightly.

How better to honor, not only her husband's memory, but the memory of all the servicemen that never made it home to hold their wives, their daughters, their sisters, their mothers.

Acknowledgements

It has been my sole intention to ensure that this book reveals a historically correct version of the events that unfolded in Vietnam between August 30, 1966 and April 11, 1967. With this said I would like to thank the Weider History Group, who without reservation allowed me access and permission to use historically correct excerpts originally published in Armchair General Magazine 'A Vietnam War Timeline' throughout my book for historical collaboration with dated love letters. Also used for historical documentation were declassified CIA documents housed in the Lyndon Baines Johnson library and excerpts from the recently released, public domain, Pentagon Papers.

The research required to complete this project was time consuming, emotional and intense. It's important to thank the many people who helped me along my journey.

I would like to thank Jim Vinson, USMC Co. D 1st Bat, 7th Marine Reg, 1st Mar Div. 67/68 for his invaluable assistance in finding the "un-findable" as my secret squirrel operative. Jim Vinson's unit received the 'Meritorious Unit Commendation' for actions in battle in Happy Valley, Quang Nam Province near the base of hill 41 against an estimated 100 Viet Cong and North Vietnamese regulars.

The pictures of James Dennis Piper on the Washington D.C. Vietnam Memorial Wall were given to me by Marine Ric Ryan (Vietnam 66/67 9th Engineer Battalion)when he fulfilled one of the dreams on his bucket list by visiting the Vietnam Wall with his wife and sons in April 2011. Not only did Ric supply me with photos, he took it upon himself to frame the original photos for Jim Piper's widow, Micki; the photos now proudly adorn the wall of her local business, along with photos of other 'local American heroes' past and present.

And what book could go to print without the keen eyes of editors and those who volunteered to critique? A thank you to Professor Judy Hewett, Investigator John Blackburn, and friend Christine Brousseau for catching the little and not so little mistakes, helping to make the book the best it could be.

I also want to note the unwavering support of my family; my husband John, my children Chris, Nick, Amanda, and Marshall, my daughters-in-law Avonlea and Kendra, my precious grand-daughter Kadence, and the support of my community, when my whole world revolved around Jim Piper and a piece of history that our country has sadly and regrettably, quietly filed away.

Lastly, and most importantly, I would like to thank Micki for sharing this incredibly personal and painful part of her life, so that "our children will not forget the past."

Please read the following pages with the understanding that Jim was from an era where sensationalism and graphic violence was not shared with spouses, children and family at home. There are only a few rare glimpses into the horrors he witnessed while serving in Vietnam. His words show the strong need for family and friends, each letter from home a lifeline to sanity, a hope for a future, a reason to survive just one more day.

Table of Contents

James Dennis Piper

Private First Class

A CO, 1ST BN, 8TH CAV RGT, 1 CAV DIV

Army of the United States

28 April 1947 - 11 April 1967

San Lorenzo, CA

James Dennis Piper was born to Bud and Betty Piper on April 28, 1947 in the small northern California town of San Lorenzo. He was the oldest of four boys.

As a proud member of the San Lorenzo High School class of '65 Jim was involved in many sports. As a freshman he was on the baseball, swimming and wrestling teams, acting as swim team manager that year. He continued football his sophomore year and became a member of the Block SL club his sophomore, junior and senior years in high school, proudly displaying his Varsity Block Letters on his letterman sweater.

A love of music led him towards becoming a drummer, an interest that eventually led him to his wife. Jim met his wife Michelle (Micki) when he was 16 years-old. He was performing with his band 'the Galaxies' at a Hawaiian Club in Oakland California called the Hui Kamaina (come a i na) when he first met Micki. According to Micki she recalls making the first move.

Jim and Micki dated their junior and senior years in high school, not letting the fact that Micki attended a high school on the other side of town sway their commitment to each other. Engaged soon after high school, Jim and Micki married June 18, 1966. Jim received his draft notice one-mere month after their vows were taken and he reported to the Armed Forces of the United States Local Board No. 54 in Hayward, California on August 30, 1966 at 6:45 A.M. where he was forwarded to the Armed Forces Induction Station in Oakland, California.

April 4, 1967

Dearest Darling,

Today is a day that I can feel nothing else to talk about except our love.

Sweetheart, I know we were made for each other, just as the moon was made for the sky.

Without the moon to light the sky at night, there would be nothing but dark, lonely emptiness. And just as you were meant for me and I for you, without your love to brighten my life, I too would be wandering about in a sea of darkness. I would never have the opportunity to see the light of love and true devotion if it were not for you my darling.

During the short time we have actually been man and wife to each other, I have felt so much of love and the wonderful feeling you get when it is shared equally.

Our lives now face the strange and new excitement of a new member to our lives. A small joy of having this wonderful miracle happen to us would be the ultimate possession of the love that binds forever our lives.

Darling do you realize the wonderful experience that we are about to encounter? Having a baby join in on the love we have for each other and the love and attention that we both can generate into caring for our child could only be gifted to those who deserve the happiness that only God himself can give.

To believe in the feeling of true love is the most time consuming and most rewarding to anyone such as we have experienced... How was that for a love letter? ...Every once in awhile I get a very strong urge to write words of love to my one and only love.

I must close now because it is getting dark. I will write again soon.

My love is all for you.

Jim

I love you Mrs. Piper.

Till death do us part in about 100 years.

Your hubby.

Jim Piper wrote that letter in anticipation of his upcoming leave, where he was to meet his young wife Michelle (Micki) on the beautiful island of Hawaii. His letter was full of a young husband's hopes and dreams for their future together, the family they would create, and the love that would last a lifetime.

That was Jim's last love letter.

PFC James Dennis Piper was killed in action on April 11, 1967, in a country a world away, in a war we should never forget.

This is not only Jim's story; it is the story of so many others that fought before him, after him, and beside him: the fathers, brothers, sons, and husbands whose lives were cut short but whose memories will live on forever in the hearts of the loved ones left behind.

Setting the stage...

March 1950: President Harry Truman approved a National Security Council (NSC) Memorandum 64 proclaiming that the French Indochina (Vietnam, Cambodia, and Laos) was a key area that could not be allowed to fall to the communists and that the United States would provide support against communist aggression in the area.

1962: US Air Force began the use of Agent Orange - a defoliant that came in metal orange containers-to expose roads and trails used by Vietcong forces.

August 1964: North Vietnamese attacked two U.S. destroyers sitting in international waters; the incident became known as the Gulf of Tonkin Incident. In response to that incident the Gulf of Tonkin resolution was approved by Congress authorizing President Lyndon Baines Johnson to "take all necessary measures to repel any armed attack against forces of the United States and to prevent further aggression." The resolution passed unanimously in the House and a margin of 82-2 in the Senate allowing Johnson full use of conventional U.S. military force in Southeast Asia without a formal declaration of war from Congress.

March 2, 196:5 Operation Rolling Thunder commenced - a sustained aerial bombing campaign of North Vietnam.

March 8, 1965: the first combat troops arrived in Vietnam.

By December 1968: U.S. troops in Vietnam reached 540,000.

March 29, 1973: the last U.S. Troops were withdrawn from Vietnam.

April 30, 1975: South Vietnam surrendered to the Communists.

November 13, 1982: the Vietnam Wall was dedicated in Washington D.C.

Armed Forces Induction – The Draft Notice

Jim Piper's draft notice arrived in the mail in late July of 1966.

The notice dated July 19, 1966 notified James Dennis Piper that he was 'hereby ordered for induction into the Armed Forces of the United States, and to report at Local Board No. 54, 24800 Mission Blvd., Hayward, California on August 30, 1966 at 6:45 A.M. for forwarding to an Armed Forces Induction Station.'

The honeymoon was over.

SELECTIVE SERVICE SYSTEM

Approval Not Required.

ORDER TO REPORT FOR INDUCTION

The President of the United States,

To James Dennis Piper
190 Sunset Blvd. Apt. 23
Hayward, Calif.   94541

LOCAL BOARD NO. 54
Alameda County
24800 Mission Blvd.
Hayward, California
94544
(LOCAL BOARD STAMP)

July 19, 1966
(Date of mailing)

SELECTIVE SERVICE NO.			
4	54	47	1230

GREETING:

You are hereby ordered for induction into the Armed Forces of the United States, and to report

at ......Local Board No. 54...... 24800 Mission Blvd.,....Hayward, California......
(Place of reporting).

on ....August 30, 1966...... at ....6:45 A.M.......
(Date)   (Hour)

for forwarding to an Armed Forces Induction Station.

To report direct to
Induction Station in
Oakland, Call 582-5456

............M.W.Lewis............
(Member or clerk of Local Board)

IMPORTANT NOTICE
(Read Each Paragraph Carefully)

IF YOU HAVE HAD PREVIOUS MILITARY SERVICE, OR ARE NOW A MEMBER OF THE NATIONAL GUARD OR A RESERVE COMPONENT OF THE ARMED FORCES, BRING EVIDENCE WITH YOU. IF YOU WEAR GLASSES, BRING THEM. IF MARRIED, BRING PROOF OF YOUR MARRIAGE. IF YOU HAVE ANY PHYSICAL OR MENTAL CONDITION WHICH, IN YOUR OPINION, MAY DISQUALIFY YOU FOR SERVICE IN THE ARMED FORCES, BRING A PHYSICIAN'S CERTIFICATE DESCRIBING THAT CONDITION, IF NOT ALREADY FURNISHED TO YOUR LOCAL BOARD.

Valid documents are required to substantiate dependency claims in order to receive basic allowance for quarters. Be sure to take the following with you when reporting to the induction station. The documents will be returned to you. (a) FOR LAWFUL WIFE OR LEGITIMATE CHILD UNDER 21 YEARS OF AGE—original, certified copy or photostat of a certified copy of marriage certificate, child's birth certificate, or a public or church record of marriage issued under the signature and seal of the custodian of the church or public records; (b) FOR LEGALLY ADOPTED CHILD—certified court order of adoption; (c) FOR CHILD OF DIVORCED SERVICE MEMBER (Child in custody of person other than claimant)—(1) Certified or photostatic copies of receipts from custodian of child evidencing serviceman's contributions for support, and (2) Divorce decree, court support order or separation order; (d) FOR DEPENDENT PARENT—affidavits establishing that dependency.

Bring your Social Security Account Number Card. If you do not have one, apply at nearest Social Security Administration Office. If you have life insurance, bring a record of the insurance company's address and your policy number. Bring enough clean clothes for 3 days. Bring enough money to last 1 month for personal purchases.

This Local Board will furnish transportation, and meals and lodging when necessary, from the place of reporting to the induction station where you will be examined. If found qualified, you will be inducted into the Armed Forces. If found not qualified, return transportation and meals and lodging when necessary, will be furnished to the place of reporting.

You may be found not qualified for induction. Keep this in mind in arranging your affairs, to prevent any undue hardship if you are not inducted. If employed, inform your employer of this possibility. Your employer can then be prepared to continue your employment if you are not inducted. To protect your right to return to your job if you are not inducted, you must report for work as soon as possible after the completion of your induction examination. You may jeopardize your reemployment rights if you do not report for work at the beginning of your next regularly scheduled working period after you have returned to your place of employment.

Willful failure to report at the place and hour of the day named in this Order subjects the violator to fine and imprisonment. Bring this Order with you when you report.

If you are so far from your own local board that reporting in compliance with this Order will be a serious hardship, go immediately to any local board and make written request for transfer of your delivery for induction, taking this Order with you.

SSS Form 252 (Revised 4-25-65)   (Previous printings may be used until exhausted.)   U. S. GOVERNMENT PRINTING OFFICE 1965 O—785-191

Leaving Home
And
Basic Training /
Ft. Lewis, Washington

August 30, 1966

To

November 4, 1966

Co B 5th Bn 2nd BDE U.S.A.T.C.

Chapter One

AUGUST & SEPTEMBER 1966

"Boy, your pork chops are 1000% better than the Army."

August 30, 1966

Hi Honey,

This jet is something extra. After we leveled off the stewardess came by with coffee.

The take off was fast and the pressure in the plane hurt our ears for awhile. The view is beautiful, even at night.

I saw you and mom and dad and Tom at the window. I, Dale and Duane were sitting right over the wing on the right side.

I wish you could be here with me on the plane. You'd love it. And besides I miss you terribly already.

Say hello to everyone for me and tell them I am doing fine.

....Oh! We're going 600 MPH. It would be quite a race for the Malibu!
More later...

We arrived in Seattle-Tacoma International Airport about 12:50. Then we took a bus to Ft. Lewis.

We got up for breakfast about 6:30 and had five minutes to eat. I don't know how I'm going to gain weight like that.

This letter may be held up for a couple of days so pay attention to the date of the mailing.

From what I can see of it, the country up here is beautiful. But our Corporal said that we won't be doing much sight-seeing.

After breakfast this morning we came back to the barracks and this is where we've been most of the day. I haven't even got my hair cut yet.

There won't be any point in writing to me until I find my permanent base. Theres all kinds of phone booths so I might call soon.

Sorry, I have to go now but I'll write again soon. I love you.

                    Your darling,
                    Jim

August 30 1966: Hanoi Radio announced that Deputy Premier Le Thank Nghi had signed an agreement with Peking whereby the People's Republic of China would provide additional economic and technical aid to North Vietnam.

(From February through August 1966 the total death toll of Viet Cong from ARVN and US Forces had reached 17,692. The death toll for the 'Free World Forces' reached 2,135 with 236 captured.)

August 1966: government documents stated that the Viet Cong claimed to have 15, 085 guerillas (including 2,990 women), 34, 441 militia (including 6.147 women), and 719 secret guerillas in the Binh Dinh Province alone.

September 1, 1966: United Nations Secretary General U Thant stated that he would not seek re-election because U.N efforts in Vietnam had failed.

September 3, 1966

Hi Honey,

Well the Army isn't too bad of a life when there's no other choice.

Thursday we got our hair cut and some shots. I've had plenty of shots in my life but nothing as potent as the yellow fever shot. So I guess you know what happened; they had to give me oxygen to bring me back. I was out cold and I don't know how long.

Gee, it was great talking to you on the phone but it costs an extra $3.00 and some odd cents for fourteen minutes. I won't be able to make very many of them but I will call again sometime during the next eight weeks.

...

Boy am I tired. I had Fire Guard Duty last night and didn't get to bed until 1:00 AM. Then we got up at 5:00 AM.

I sure am out of shape. Yesterday 2 of us ran 2 ½ to 3 miles without stopping and I'm sore.

Well so far this is like an eight hour job only 12 hours long. We start at 5:30 A.M. and end at 5:30 P.M. Then we get the rest of the night off unless someone goofs up, then we gotta go out and do the job over again.

I'm already gaining weight even though I haven't been on a scale I can feel the extra weight...

Yesterday we got a partial pay of $25.00 to go to the px and buy some things we will need for basic. I haven't spent any of that yet, but I've got everything I need. I used my money I brought from home. I'm going to save as much as I can for when I come home.

I had my personal affairs taken care of and <u>this is important</u> I had to claim you and myself on the income tax form because I am now in the service. So when you have the income tax to fill out this year please don't forget. Its very important.

You also get $95.20 from the government: $55.20 from them and $40.00 from me.

We had an inspection today with a four star General and man I was scared.

I didn't have to salute him because we were told not to but also today we were cleaning up the area around the barracks and I had as arm load of weeds and a lieutenant walked up to me right after I dumped them in the trash can. I didn't see him until I turned around. I was told not to salute an officer and I couldn't go around him without displaying some type of military courtesy so I saluted him. He said, "Good morning trooper, very good salute, carry on." Boy was I relieved. I kind of felt pretty good too because he was the officer who told us not to salute. That was because we didn't know how but I think I passed the supreme test. Our Sergeant taught all of us how to salute about an hour before.

I love you.

Your hubby,

Me

P.S. Your I.D. for the PX should be coming in the mail shortly, please make good use of it, because everything in the PX is cheaper.

September 4, 1966: search and destroy operation Baton Rouge began in the southern portion of the Rung Sat Special Zone to secure the water line of communication between the port of Saigon and the East China Sea. The operation destroyed 59 sampans and 50 base camp locations.

September 6, 1966

Hi Sweetheart,

Looking at your picture all day long makes me homesick. I wish I could be with you for an hour or two.

Now that I am completely processed I'll start basic on the 12th of September. So far I've had it real easy. My orders for platoon squad leader are not in yet, but I expect them anytime now. Its kinda fun being an acting Corporal...I'm getting full respect, cooperation and admiration from all my men.

Staying here for one week sure makes me realize how much I truly love you and miss you so terribly. I didn't want to tell you, but on the plane I went into the bathroom and cried my heart out.

...

I've got a surprise for you when I get home. It's very good so don't worry about what kind it is. I'm not real positive myself, but if my test scores look as good as the Sergeant told me I've got a good chance. Tell everyone I'll be home either Nov 7 or Nov 8 depending on if I can get a flight. I'll know for sure around Halloween. I might be home for your birthday because I have a fifteen day leave.

...

I love you with all of my lonely little heart.
Your loving husband
Jim

September 10, 1966

My dearest Darling,

...I received your letter yesterday and just had time today to write back.

I read it and got all choked up. All the guys know I was wishing I could be with you so they left me alone and didn't bother me for awhile. Honey I miss you so much I feel like sitting down and dying. Everything will start getting tough on Monday. I wish you could see how funny I look with a helmet and rifle.

I wish I could have been home for the barbequed chicken. This Army chow is good but not as good as yours honey. All day long we've been marching and having clean up duties. It seems like all my energy is going to waste.

...

I'll close with all the many, many kisses I've saved up ..

Yours everlasting,

Jim

September 10th and 11[th,] *1966: during South Vietnam's elections, there were 166 Viet Cong acts of terrorism just before and during election day; fifteen times the level of activity on an average day in August. US forces were in place to act as a shield to prevent large-scale VC and NVA interference. Approximately 81% of the population turned out to vote.*

September 12, 1966

Dearest Love,

...

All hell broke loose today because it was the first day of Basic.

Even as squad leader I still have to go through basic training and its getting pretty rough now. ..I'm writing to you when I should be polishing my extra pair of boots...I may be writing more often, but the letters will be a little shorter.

...

I miss you so terribly much that I sometimes don't know what to do next. Your letters are wonderful...say, if you start swimming in your tears, I'll start swimming in mine and I'll meet you half way. OK!

...

I know what you mean when you say you take me to bed with you mentally because my buddy squad leader tells me every night "not to take you to bed with me" because "women aren't allowed on the post."

This will have to be closed for now honey. Remember that I'll always remain true as I was when I left.

All my everlasting and unending love,

Jim

P.S. I LOVE YOU MUCH!

September 12, 1966: five hundred US Air Force planes bombed enemy supply lines and coastal targets in North Vietnam in the heaviest air raid of the war.

September 12, 1966: US intelligence appraisal of the bombing of North Vietnam with emphasis on oil storage sites, lines of communications and transportation equipment stated, 'There is no evidence of oil shortage, of transport problems, or of weakened public morale; however, measurable damage to the economy now stands at $125 million.'

...

September 13, 1966:

> ➢ *Westmoreland discussed build-up in Quang Tri Province. Requested authority to use B-52 strikes.*

> ➢ *1ˢᵗ Cav Div launches 40 day search and destroy Operation Thayer 1 in Binh Dinh Province.*

...

September 14, 1966: U.S. II Field Forces initiated Operation Attleboro an attack by the 196th Light Infantry Brigade against Viet Cong forces near the Cambodian Border in War Zone C (near Tay Ninh, 50 miles northwest of Saigon in III Corps Tactical Zone).

...

September 15, 1966: Operation Deckhouse IV was conducted by the SLF (Special Landing Force) as an adjunct to operation Prairie. Deckhouse IV officially ended on the 18th, but the BLT (Battalion Landing Team) stayed in support of Prairie until the 25th. The operation claimed at least 200 NVA killed at a cost of 36 US KIA and 167 US WIA.

September 16, 1966

Hi Honey,

...I'm sure glad I called you tonight. It's so good hearing your voice again. I'll call next Thursday at 8:00 P.M. I can't promise that I can get through to you though. Every time I try to call the long distance lines are filled up.

Honey, when I get home you're going to laugh at me. I told you tonight that I got another haircut but you've got to see it to believe it. The length of my longest hair is all of 1/8 of an inch...

Today is the fourth day of training. That means only 52 more before we graduate. It won't be long because it seems like only yesterday that I left and it's been 16 days since I last held you in my arms. That's a long time but its passing quickly I think...

I hope you will be able to come with me where ever I go from the time I get out of basic. You might not be able to for the first couple of months because of schooling...

That old saying about lover's being separated is true. "Absence makes the heart grow fonder." And it does. I didn't think I could miss anyone as much as I miss you and not being able to be with you constantly...

I don't know why I have the luck of being loved and married to the most thoughtful, understanding woman in the world. I know guys who would die to even get a look at you...

How can anyone have a ball in the Army is far beyond me. It may sound like fun the way its being written but believe me this is no place for a lazy man. The hours are ridiculous, 5:00 A.M. till 9:00 P.M. Then extra duty on top of that. No thank you...Some of these people haven't got enough brains to be stupid...

They're treating me rough but its not terrible. I've been eating regular, but they don't give you enough to eat. Its just enough to hold you over until the next meal...

I love you with all my heart.

Your everlasting love,
Jim
P.S. I LOVE YOU MUCH!

September 16, 1966: Operation Golden Fleece 7-1 began, designed to protect the rice harvest, with the single Marine battalion from operation Fresno operating in the Mo Duc District.

September 18, 1966

Hi Darling,

Happy Anniversary! Bet you thought I wouldn't remember. Well today we passed inspection. And it seemed like I held my breath all the time. We had three inspections in 2 days. I sure hope there won't be any more. Today after I finish this letter I'm going to polish my boots and call you if I get a chance...

Sweety, I've said a hundred times that I miss you but each time I say it I know the next time I'll miss you more. It keeps getting worse every day. I feel so bad having to leave you so soon after we've been married. But the sooner I get this over with the better off I'll be and you too. When I think of it that way, I feel much better, don't you?...

I think the names you have picked out for our children are great. For twins I like: Annet Marie Piper and Lynett Marie Piper...

Boy, your pork chops are 1000% better than the Army. They were fried so crisp it was like biting into wood. Their mashed potatoes I could have eaten with a straw they were so runny. It was about the worst meal I've ever eaten...

I will see you in 6 weeks and 5 days from today. Depending on the time I get a flight to San Francisco. With everyone graduating at the same time it's going to be first come first serve at the airport. I hope I'm first...

Darling I wish I could find a way to express my love for you in a letter but I can't. I've got so much on my mind and in my heart to tell you but the feeling of expressed love just won't go in a letter. All I can do is talk about it and let it go at that until I can once again hold you in my arms. Then I will be able to express this beautiful feeling of deep, rich love that I have swelling up within my heart every second that I am away from you...Every time I write a letter I feel that I am always leaving something out. Or that I have failed to put all my love into every letter of the alphabet. But darling I am trying harder to let you know how much I miss you and love you. I'll never leave you honey, just be patient and I'll be home soon.

The love of your life,
Jim
P.S. You're the only love of mine.

September 18/19, 1966

Hi Darling,

I'm still writing. It seems like I can't stop thinking about you even for a minute. Today we went to the PX and I got everything I need for the next 8 weeks. All I need now is you. For nothing I buy no matter how expensive will take the place of my love for you.

Every night this week I've laid awake in bed and thought of how we met and all the good times we've had together before and after we were married. Too bad we can't have any of those good times right now.

I won't be able to make any phone calls this week because one guy made a phone call last night after curfew and so now no one can make any calls for a week...

On my P.T. (physical training) test I got an official 392 points and you need 300 to qualify. The Sergeant told us squad leaders that if we didn't make the qualification he would take our stripes away from us. Well, I have to do some typing for the Sergeant so I will continue this letter tomorrow...

I haven't done any typing in a long time so I'm back to writing a letter again, the Sergeant seems to think I make too many mistakes. He's right. I typed ten lines and made 6 mistakes. ..

As I was saying before I did the typing. I qualified and got to keep my stripes. But the Platoon guide he has Sergeant stripes and he didn't qualify. He only had 222 points. ..

Honey, right now I don't know what your chances of going with me right away are. Because I might have M.P. school and you wouldn't be able to go with me there or I might have Advanced Individual Training and you can't go there but I'll have to wait for my orders to come through before I know for sure...

I miss you and love you very much darling . Please write again soon. I'll have to close for now.

My love always,
Jim

September 19, 1966:

> ➤ *Johnson administrations' handling of the war came under attack by a group of 22 eminent scientists, including seven Nobel laureates urging the President to halt the use of antipersonnel and anti-crop chemical weapons in Vietnam.*

> ➤ *House Republicans issued a "White Paper" that warned that the United States was becoming "a full-fledged combatant" in a war that was becoming "bigger than the Korean War." The paper urged the President to end the war "more speedily and at a smaller cost, while safeguarding the independence and freedom of South Vietnam."*

> ➤ *Johnson's handling of the war was also questioned in the United Nations, where Secretary General U Thant proposed a three-point plan for peace in Vietnam, which included cessation of U.S. bombing of the North; de-escalation of the ground war in South Vietnam; and inclusion of the National Liberation Front in the Paris peace talks.*

> ➤ *In Rome, Pope Paul VI appealed to world leaders in a papal encyclical to end the Vietnam War. Despite such calls, the United States launched extensive bombing raids by B-52s that lasted for four days against a mixture of targets in the DMZ, including infiltration trails, troop concentrations, supply areas, and base camps.*

September 22, 1966: Arthur J. Goldberg, U.S. Representative to the United Nations, statement before the U.N. General Assembly, under the Pentagon heading 'Justification of the War.'

"Our affirmative aims in Viet-Nam.

It is because of the attempt to upset by violence the situation in Viet-Nam, and its far-reaching implications elsewhere, that the United States and other countries have responded to appeals from South Viet-Nam for military assistance."

Our aims in giving this assistance are strictly limited.

We are not engaged in a 'holy war' against communism.

We do not seek to establish an American empire or a sphere of influence in Asia.

We seek no permanent military bases, no permanent establishment of troops, no permanent alliances, no permanent American presence of any kind in South Viet-Nam.

We do not seek to impose a policy of alignment on South Viet-Nam.

We do not seek to overthrow the Government of North Viet-Nam.

We do not seek to do any injury to mainland China nor to threaten any of its legitimate interests.

We do not ask of North Viet-Nam an unconditional surrender or indeed the surrender of anything that belongs to it.

Nor do we seek to exclude any segment of the South Vietnamese people from peaceful participation in their country's future.

Let me state affirmatively and succinctly what our aims are.

We want a political solution, not a military solution, to this conflict. By the same token, we reject the idea that North Viet-Nam has the right to impose a military solution.

We seek to assure the people of South Viet-Nam the same right of self-determination – to decide its own political destiny, free of force—that the United Nations Charter affirms for all.

And we believe that reunification of Viet-Nam should be decided upon through a free choice by the peoples of both the North and the South without outside interference, the results of which choice we are fully prepared to support."

September 22, 1966: the ROK (Republic of Korea) Capital Division conducted operation MAENG HO 9 in Binh Dinh Province, claiming 1,161 known enemy casualties. (PFC James Piper was killed in action in Binh Dinh Province 7 months later.)

September 23, 1966: the Battle for Mutter's ridge took place, 3rd Battalion, 4th Marines, at a cost of six Marines and fifty enemy, the Americans controlled Hill 400 by the afternoon.

September 24, 1966

Dear Sweetheart,

I know it's been too long between letters but I haven't had much time to myself this week.

That bit of information that draftees can't take their wives with them better not be true. As far as I know you can go with me...

I just received your first two letters yesterday. They were miss-sent to the reception station and they just now got to me. That 29 page letter was long but great...Everybody asked me if I was going to publish it because it was so long...

I had my picture taken but it will be awhile before I get the picture back from being developed. As soon as I do I'll send it to you. I've got my helmet on and my arm-band but I've got my boots off so it looks like I'm real comfortable...

You better sit down for this. I heard today, but its not for sure, that my whole company might not have leave after basic so that I'll be able to come home for Christmas. That's not bad, but I want to see you as soon as possible. Only 41 days to go...

Today we have another inspection by the Major. We have to dress in our dress uniform and be spic and span in appearance. I put on my dress uniform last night and it looks real sharp except the sleeves are too short. I'll have to get it altered.

Well my darling...please write back soon. I'll always wait for you, believe me. It's the only thought I have that keeps me going. ..

With deep devotion and unending love I remain,

Jim

September 25, 1966

Hi Sweetheart,

...Next week we start firing our rifles. I just got two more guys in my squad that got recycled because they didn't pass the marksmanship test. They only had two more weeks to graduate; now they have to go through it again. I sure feel sorry for them but they are kind of goofy. They don't look very bright. I hope I don't get recycled anywhere around here if I do...

It made me feel good to know that I can be home on Christmas and New Years with you. We haven't missed one year in three years and the first one we were going steady, the second one we were engaged and now the third one we are married, so I really didn't want to miss one at all.

Another thing I heard today is that draftees will not go to Viet Nam because the tour of duty last 13 months and in order to go to Viet Nam we have to have 11 months of training and 3 months of leave during those 2 years and 3 months of R&R after we get back. R&R is rest and relaxation at Army cost. So that the Army would have to keep us 30 months and its too expensive. The Government can't afford it if it keeps us in.

Well honey it's time to spit shine my boots for tomorrow and take a shower. Please write back soon.

I love you with all my heart. You are always on my mind constantly. Tell me you love me in every letter even though I know it

All my love and passion,
Jim

September 27, 1966

Hi Sweetie,

...tomorrow we'll go to the rifle range to "sight in" our weapons. We will be there all day and for the next 3 days...

I'm not sure but I think we have 91 days before Christmas and only 82 days before I can be rejoined with you. Actually to see you at Christmas is the best present I could receive...

Well I'm going to have to close for now because I'm out of writing paper and I've only got 2 sheets left and I don't know when I can get to the PX.

I love you so much that my heart is about to bust wide open...I'll write again soon.

All my love, believe me,

Jim

September 29, 1967: according to intelligence reports there were an estimated total of 25,000 to 45,000 Chinese support troops in North Vietnam.

September 30, 1966

Hi Honey,

I received your cookies today and they were delicious as you will soon find out. These are some of the guys in the platoon who sampled them:

(see image next page)

Honey there were many others that tried them but I don't have any more paper but they all raved about them just like I said they would. The first foreign language written above is galic from the guy from Ireland. The second is Spanish and they mean thank you very much. They were so delicious I wish there was more. Thanks for the cigs too because I sure needed them. I miss you too sweetheart and love you very much. I know I'm going to get fat when I get out.

I'll write a long letter soon maybe tomorrow after inspection. I love you.

Heres all my love for you.

Jim

FORT LEWIS
Washington

30, Sept 66

Hi honey,

I received your cookies today and they were delicious as you will soon find out.

These are some of the guys in the platoon who sampled them:

Ken Allen

Jerell Woodword

Mary Crosston

Craig Wick

Robert Woosun (Very delicious)

Gary Denton " "

Johnny Doyle

George Bean

Bob Foster

Tell Grandma the nuts were good too. Jim.

Steve Warbick (they were Great!)) Please send

Mickey Zimmerman very good   MORE

Bruce Neill really good

Dan Hill

Dan Beete

Joseph B. Dominguez   Thank you very much.

Steve Gilead - "They were very good thank you"
the "Loosl" My Dad was Jim's Boss at G.F.
George Guy. Thank you very much.
(Go Raig míle maíc agac.)
Stan Perkins thank you very much.
(Muy gracias por los galetas)
EARLE Miller - THANK YOU VERY MUCH

Honey there were many others who tried them but I don't have any more paper but they all raved about them just like I said they would. The first foreign language written above is Galic from the guy from Ireland. The second is Spanish and they mean Thank you very much. They were so delicious I wish there was smore. Thanks for the Cigs too because I sure needed them. I miss you too, sweetheart and love you very much. I know I'm going to get fat when I finally get out.

I'll write a long letter soon maybe tomorrow after inspection. I love you.

Heres all my love for you.

Jim.

In a memo to President Johnson the DCI (Director of Counter Intelligence) stated that bombing of North Vietnam had produced about 29,000 total casualties (killed and injured) from the beginning of the Rolling Thunder program in February 1965 through September 1966. About 11,000 were military and 18,000 were logistics workers and other civilians.

Chapter Two

OCTOBER 1966

"...when I go to bed at night I pretend you are there with your soft skin touching mine and keeping me warm."

October 1, 1966: Proposal from Lodge (Ambassador to South Vietnam '63-'67) sets a piaster (standard money unit of South Vietnam) ceiling of 42 billion on military spending in South Vietnam.

October 2, 1966:

➢ *The Soviet Defense Ministry newspaper, Krasnaya Zuezda, reported that Russian military experts had come under fire during U.S. raids against North Vietnamese missile sites while the Soviets were training North Vietnamese soldiers in the use of Soviet-made anti-aircraft missiles. This was the first public acknowledgement that Soviets had trained North Vietnamese missile crews. Until that point both Soviets and Chinese had denied they had personnel in Vietnam.*

➢ *Operation Irving began. This operation combined elements from the 1st Cavalry Division with ARVN and ROK units mounted against the NVA Division 3 in Binh Dinh Province. The allies claimed 681 known enemy casualties and 2,000 prisoners of war at the time of completion October 24, 1966.*

October 3, 1966:

> ➤ *The Soviet Union announced it would provide military and economic assistance to North Vietnam.*

> ➤ *GVN (Government of the Republic of Vietnam) officials rejected peace negotiations with Viet Cong as separate party.*

October 4, 1966: Pope Paul VI addressed 150,000 people in St. Peter's square in Rome calling for an end to the war in Vietnam through negotiations.

October 5, 1966: the Battle for Mutter's Ridge began again following an early morning air strike, the enemy left behind ten bodies and numerous blood trails that marked the evacuation of many wounded. The battle for the ridge was finally over, with the Third Battalion, Fourth Marines driving the NVA 324B Division back into the DMZ, losing twenty dead but killing one hundred enemy.

It was during the battle of Mutter's Ridge that photographer Larry Burroughs took this picture, one of the most famous photographs of the Vietnam War.

October 6, 1966

My Darling Wife,

I received three of your letters in 2 days and was excited as you probably know to open and read every word. I enjoy reading your letters so very much.

No my cold is not much better, in fact I got a sore throat to go with it.

...The fellas really enjoyed receiving your letter. All of them did get a big kick out of it.

Well, I don't know what I want for Christmas other than to see you and hold you in my arms once again. That would be the biggest present I could have right at the moment and <u>forever after</u>.

...Did you get your allotment check yet? If not, let me know right away so I can get it straightened out. I hope you aren't too tied down with bills. I feel so guilty leaving you with all of them.

...Next week the training schedule is really rough. We are going to be doing everything we learned in the past 4 weeks.

...I know what you mean when you said every night your thoughts are of me. My thoughts are of you every minute of the day. And when I go to bed at night I pretend you are there with your soft warm skin touching mine and keeping me warm.

I love you
Much
Jim

October 6, 1966

Hi Honey,

This will be a very short letter but it has pictures in it and they say that pictures contain 2,000 words. You know that every one of those words says "I love you," over and over again.

...The one of the "Three Stooges" is about the best one I'm in. Luseretta is the guy whos father I worked for at General Foods.

...I'll try to write more soon.

Remember I'll always love you. Don't forget that please.

All my love,

Jim

P.S. Write soon.   Your love.

Jim

October 9, 1966

Hi honey,

  ...Only 69 more days and I'll be home for you and the holidays. Isn't that great? I'm counting the days right now, but I'm looking forward to counting the seconds.
  ...I sure miss you honey. I want you with me so bad. I wish you could send me more pictures of yourself. I've got three now but I don't keep them with me all the time cause I might lose them so I leave them in the barracks. I want at least one snapshot I can show to the other platoons so I can brag about my baby.
  ...With caressing love,
     Jim

October 11, 1966

My dearest deepest love,

 ...Today we went to the rifle range to qualify in order to pass basic and not have to take basic over again. I passed but just barely. I'm kind of glad because it lowers my chances of going to Viet Nam.

 ...Darling, I know what you are going through without me home but you should be in my place. It's like jail here. They take all of your rights away from you and then give <u>some</u> back as privileges. Big deal. I'd rather have my freedom. Sometimes when I feel like going to the bathroom they tell me to hold it until I bust open so they can practice first aid on me. Or when I feel like going to the PX all by myself to get personal items they tell me what to buy, how much to spend and when to spend it.

 You really don't get enough to eat to fill you up. Just enough to get you by. No seconds. That's terrible.

 ...I love you darling and I can't wait to see you in December so I can start right from <u>scratch</u> loving you again. How are you doing without me to help you?

 I love you with all my heart and pride.

 All my caressing love,

  Jim

October 12, 1966: the New York Times reported that 40% of U.S. economic aid sent to Saigon is stolen or winds up on the black market.

Picture of US aid in village black market.

October 13, 1966: Defense Secretary Robert S. McNamara, on his eighth fact finding mission to Saigon, declared at a news conference that military operations had "progressed very satisfactorily since 1965." Though later he revealed privately to President Johnson that he thought progress was "very slow indeed" in the pacification program.

October 14, 1966:

> ➤ *Secretary of Defense recommended force levels at 470,000, that US stabilize Rolling Thunder, deploy a barrier and gird itself for a long haul.*

> ➤ *Joint Chiefs of Staff did not agree with the Secretary of Defense 470,000 man limitation and are doubtful on feasibility of barrier.*

October 15, 1966

Hi darling,

...The reason we have so many inspections is beyond me. I think its just part of harassment and something to do. We have to get a haircut each week. After this week we can finally start letting it grow out.

...I know that you would adore having a child and I sure would be a proud father. Yes honey I _really_ do want to be a father. I want to be a father right now...DO you think I could ever make a responsible father? I'll sure give it one hell of a try if you still want to let me.

All of the guys in my squad told me to tell you they've all been angels and to please send some more cookies. They sure go for them. Me too honey. I really enjoy your cookies. I liked the last batch even better. I'll bet the _next_ one will be even better (hint).

I'm sorry my boots weren't polished but I was writing a letter to you during pre-inspection but the Sergeant said that they looked fine so I continued writing my letter. When the final inspection came the Lieutenant checked me for it. Its no big sweat so don't worry.

Boy I sure am tired of seeing the same scenery every day. All these dingy looking barracks and everyone wearing the same clothes day in and day out.

We only have 20 days to go before we graduate from basic. I wish it were only 20 days before I could come home. I only have 62 days before I come home or 8 weeks and 6 days. I'm more than half way there.

The hardest part of basic is yet to come. When I go on Bivouac you probably won't be able to get any letters from me for about 4 days. Don't worry though when I get back I'll have plenty to tell you. We probably won't go for another two weeks. I don't think I'm going to enjoy marching 15 miles to the Bivouac sight with a full field pack. When we get there we have to dig a fox hole and sleep in it for 3 days.

It's not going to be like camping at Lake Berryessa.

...

All my love forever,
Jim

October 15, 1966:

> ➤ *U.S. troops moved into Tay Ninh Province near the Cambodian border, approximately 50 miles north of Saigon. The purpose of the operation which began in September was to find and eliminate all enemy troops west of the Michelin rubber plantation. It was the largest U.S. operation to date involving 20,000 allied troops at the height of the fighting.*

> ➤ *During Operation Irving in Binh Dinh Province, 1st Cavalry troops found a medical cache with several thousand containers of medicine and at another location, camera equipment with 5,000 reels of film. Among the cameras found was one that belonged to Sam Castan, Look Magazine senior editor, who had been killed during Operation Crazy Horse in May. Over 1,170 prisoners were captured and identified as Viet Cong or North Vietnamese regulars during Operation Irving.*

> ➤ *In a CIA communication the CIA stated that there was little hope for a satisfactory conclusion of the war within the next two years, also stating that a US force level of 470,000 should be sufficient.*

October 16, 1966

Hi Darling,

I can't figure this Army out. They sure are being nice to us all of a sudden. We got to go to the show 2 days in a row. I didn't go though because I thought I would use this extra time to write you a nice long letter.

This morning I went to church and that was enough for me to break the monotony. I don't want to see those old reruns anyway.

(Jim proceeded to write a 5 page letter to his bride reliving their wedding day and evening, covering that romantic day with the intimate passion of young love.)

I don't think I will ever make a set novelist but I think I did alright.

Well it's raining again and it's so cold.

October 17, 1966: President Johnson left Washington for a 17-day trip to seven Asian and Pacific nations and a conference scheduled in Manila. At a stop-over in Australia he was heckled by anti-war demonstrators.

October 18, 1966:

➢ *President Johnson opened a conference in Manila with delegates from the US, South Vietnam, South Korea, the Philippines, Thailand, Australia and New Zealand.*

> *Prime Minister Nguyen Cao Ky, Minister of Information and Open Arms Nguyen Bao Tri, Director General of National Police Nguyen Ngoc Loan, and III Corps Commander General Le Nguyen Khang, accepted the resignations of Deputy Prime Minister Nguyen Luu Vien, and the Ministers of Education, Social Welfare, Youth, Communications and Transport, Labor, and Economy.*

October 19, 1966: The 196th Light Infantry Brigade on Operation Attleboro ran into major enemy forces south of Suoi Da while searching for rice and other enemy supplies. Four companies of the U. S. 5th Special Forces Group's Mobile Strike Force were inserted into landing zones north and east of Suoi Da and immediately became heavily engaged. The VC's major objective: wiping out the Special Forces camp at Suoi Da. The four Special Forces companies were overrun and withdrew in small groups or were extracted by helicopter. In response, General Westmoreland committed more infantry divisions, as the battle developed, some 22,000 US and allied troops were engaged there.

October 20, 1966: Commander in Chief US Pacific Command (CINCPAC) recommended the build-up of 91 maneuver battalions and 493,969 personnel by the end of 1967. Total strength after filling out would be 94 battalions and 555,741 personnel.(This amount exceeded the CIA's "sufficient" US force projection by 85,741 personnel.)

(The October 16, 1966 letter continues on October 20, 1966.)

I'm sorry I haven't written or sent this off earlier. I even lost my pen. They've kept me so busy. We even get to sleep until 8:30 am that's because we got off at 1:30 AM.

Monday night after I called I went back to the barracks and worked on the clean up detail.

Tuesday night we were out in the field for individual tactical training until 8:30 then we came back to the barracks and went straight to bed. Wednesday night we went back to the same place for the night phase of I.T.T.

Tonight we were out at the night firing range and right now its 12:45 A.M. But I was determined to get this letter off in the mail today. Please don't be mad because it wasn't even my fault. We haven't even had time to go to the P.X. and I am completely out of cigarettes. I've had two cigarettes all day and had to bum them off of someone in my squad. If you can, please send them to me because I still don't know when I can go to the P.X.

Today we had physical training in the rain and it started hailing. Then tonight when we were out on the firing range it began to snow. That's how cold and wet it is around here. I sure wish I was home with you so you could keep me warm. I know that I wouldn't be cold very long.

...I'm looking forward to starting a family when I get home.

Boy! I sure hope it doesn't get any colder because we go on Bivouac next week and I don't want to sleep in a wet foxhole.

I'm sorry I have to close for now but I'll try to get another letter to you tomorrow.

All of my love forever,
Jim
P.S. I'll always say I love you and I'll always mean it.

October 22, 1966: in a move intended to discredit the September 11, 1966 Government of Vietnam (GVN) elections and to create a legitimate government the formation of pseudo-democratic institutions were accelerated to build a legitimate institution.

October 23, 1966

Dearest Darling,

...Gee it was wonderful to hear your lovely voice once again, but it's still not the way I want to hear it (like in person maybe). It won't be long now before I can finally be with you. Only 57 more days and then we can go to the Christmas party together. Among other things.

...Have you seen Jimbo yet? I hear hes going to Viet Nam in a little while. If I do go there I hope to be stationed with his outfit. We could play combat together just like at Knowland Park except for real this time. Do you realize that all of the old gang is now in the service?

There's Ken – Army
Jimbo – Army
Me – Army
Abel – Air Force
Gary – Air Force
Butchie – Air Force

And we will all be getting out about the same time.

Did I tell you the Commanding Officer of my company wanted me to go to Officer Candidate School? The only thing is I have to sign up for one more year. The school lasts for 23 weeks and if I don't flunk out I'd graduate as 2nd Lieutenant with about $450.00 a month. But I flatly told him no thanks, that I was married and had a good job waiting for me when I got out...He gave me a long lecture about being proud to be in America and serve my country as a leader and he was surprised I was not very patriotic toward my country...They have already got too many Chiefs and not enough Indians. He's still not quite happy with my decision. But as I said before S.N.A.F.U. (situation normal all f----d up) I just want to come home to you and stay.

Well its raining here again and colder than hell. I hope next week clears up from Monday to Thursday and I'll be happy...

All my love everlasting,
Jim

October 24, 1966:

> ➢ *President Johnson met with Allied leaders in Manila where they pledged to withdraw troops from Vietnam within six months if North Vietnam withdrew "its forces to the North and ceased infiltration of South Vietnam." A communiqué signed by the seven participants (Australia, New Zealand, South Korea, South Vietnam, the Philippines, Thailand, and the United States) included a four-point "Declaration of Peace" that stressed the need for a "peaceful settlement of the war in Vietnam and for future peace and progress" in the rest of Asia and the Pacific.(Months after the Manila Conference Secretary of Defense John McNaughton summarized "The national commitment of the United States in South Vietnam (SVN), as stated in Manila, is that the South Vietnamese people shall not be conquered by aggressive force and shall enjoy the inherent right to choose their own way of life and their own form of government. The United States is committed to continue our military and all other efforts, as firmly and as long as be necessary, in close consultation with our allies until the aggression is ended.")*

> ➢ *Dissident montagnards (people from the mountains) pledged loyalty to GVN(Government of the Republic of Vietnam).*

October 25, 1966: Operation Thayer II began. This operation, preceded by Thayer I and followed by Pershing, was conducted by the 1st Cavalry Division in the northern coastal plain and Kim Son and Suoi Ca Valleys to the west in Binh Dinh Province claiming 1757 known enemy casualties.

October 26, 1966:

> ➤ *President Johnson visited Cam Ramh Bay, South Vietnam. After being introduced by General Westmoreland, General Thieu welcomed the President saying that this was the first time a U.S. President had visited South Vietnam. General Westmoreland was awarded the Distinguished Service Medal by President Johnson. The President continued to the base hospital and awarded the Purple Heart to all Americans in each ward.*

> ➤ *McNaughton (United States Assistant Secretary of Defense for International Security Affairs) reported a conversation with Westmoreland stating Westmoreland was thinking of an ending CY '67 strength of 480,000. (10,000 more than CIA suggested and 75,741 less than Commander in Chief US Pacific Command requested.)*

October 27, 1966: U.S. Ambassador-at-Large Averell Harriman, acting as Johnson's personal emissary, visited leaders in Ceylon, Indonesia, India, Pakistan, Iran, Italy, France, West Germany, Britain, and Morocco to explain the results of the Manila conference and the "Declaration of Peace" signed there by Allied leaders with troops in Vietnam.

October 28, 1966

Hi Darling,

I just got back from Bivouac and I'm miserably cold, wet, and dirty. I've got to wait until after 1:00 P.M. formation to take a shower.

We had sunshine Monday and Tuesday then we had a flood Wednesday. We were going through a close combat course and it started pouring. It wasn't just a little rain as usual. It really came down. When we came back our camp was soaked and we almost couldn't sleep in our sleeping bags because our tent leaked. Today we packed everything back up and came back to the barracks. We had to come home on foot and it was a force march. We went 12.3 miles in 2 ½ hours. We were really going on that march. I hope I never have to do that again.

Oh yeah, my orders came through and it's posted on the bulletin board at the Orderly room. I'm going to Fort Polk, Louisiana for my A.I.T. I don't know what my job will be or what my training will be because they won't post the personal orders. They just post where you are going.

I only have 8 more days before I graduate and I can hardly wait. We go through the infiltration course tonight where they shoot real bullets over your head with a machine gun. We have to crawl and they shoot about 40 inches off the ground. You better believe I'm going to crawl, and real low.

Only 50 days left and I'll be able to see you again and love you. You can bet your 3¢ that I'm not going to let go of you all the time I'm home. You will probably get tired of me holding you all the time.

...Darling it's time for me to close. I can't think of anymore to say except that I love you and I still want to be a father.

My love forever.

Jim

October 29, 1966

Dearest Darling,

I have thought about going to O.C.S. and even if I made Captain in 6 years I'd only make $495.00 a month. I don't like the Army. All I want to do is get out as soon as possible so I can live my life the way I want to...All I want is to be with you now. O.C.S. lasts 23 weeks and after that I would have 1 ½ year combat tour of duty so by that time I would be going home anyway. My tour of duty would be Viet Nam (guaranteed). And even if I was a General you couldn't go with me. That's enough of that. If I do decide to go I can go at a later date. We'll discuss it when I come home for Christmas. O.K.?

...I got your tape yesterday and it sure sounded boss. I like the way you put Love is a Many Splendored thing in with you talking. The Hawaiian Wedding Song really drew tears to my eyes. That was so tough I just played it over and over again. I had to turn off the tape recorder when Bay I'm Yours, came on. I had to go out and get a cigarette before I fell apart...

All my everlasting
Love,
Jim

October 29, 1966

Hi Darling,

I had a few minutes to write so I thought I would take advantage of this rare opportunity...

I hope to be home by the 17th of December. That way I can rest up and take a shower and shave before the party. I haven't been able to locate the mail clerk today to find out about your allotment check. I cornered him yesterday and I'm still trying to bug him about it. He said if you didn't get it yet you should get it pretty soon and that he would look into it. So I've been trying to find him today and I just remembered its Sunday, and there's no mail on Sunday so the mail clerk won't be in his office. I'm so mixed up I can't remember what day it is.

Only 5 more days and I don't have to look at this place anymore. You said you only have 3¢. Well consider yourself lucky because I have exactly 0¢ until Tuesday...

Boy you should see my combat boots. You wouldn't know they had been scuffed and in the rain, mud and sand by the way I've shined them. They look like patent leather. I really had to work hard on them for graduation. It's a good thing I've got 2 pair of boots.

Darling I was just thinking about starting a family and I had the most wonderful , warmest feeling I've had since I came into the service...When do you want to start? We should be able to make ends meet with the allotment check and with another dependent I should get a little more to send home. I can already hear the pitter patter of little feet. Can you knit? Well Darling we've got nine months or so to really decide on a name so why don't we concentrate on having our little bundles of joy first.

Here's a small poem that will take a lot of thinking to get the true meaning.
When recreation done
You disagree gently but reinclose softly
Your self into a pattern of singleness
As you turn from me to sleep
I wonder if you belong so much
To me as you dream, as your touch
Has made it seem...

My everlasting love,
Jim
P.S. Pray for twins.

October 29, 1966: Operation Paul Revere began. A search and destroy mission in Oasis, Du Co, Pleiku, Chu Pong, Ia Drang Valley, and Binh Dinh Province.

October 31, 1966

Hi Darling,

...We got paid today and I got $45.00. Did you get your allotment yet? I don't know why its so damn late. I know they are taking it out of my pay. I'm going to send you a money order of $25.00 to keep for me so I can come home. That way I won't spend it foolishly at the P.X. and I'll have enough to come home on for Christmas if you send it back when I need it...

Letter continues on November 1, 1966
I haven't much time, this will be a fast letter.
Tomorrow we are going to get some more shots. I think these are the last ones.
...
All of my love to you,
Jim

Chapter Three

NOVEMBER 1966

"...I really don't know if I'm going to Vietnam or not."

November 2, 1966

Dearest Darling,

Just received some great news. Today I got a letter from the Battalion Commander promoting me to Private E-2. That's Private 2nd class with a slight pay raise. By the time I get out of A.I.T. I might make E-3. That's Private First Class with another pay raise. With all good news comes a little bad. I will be going to Ft Polk immediately after graduation Nov 4 and have to report Nov 5. I will be getting training in either small mortar firing or 50 caliber machine guns. I hope that doesn't mean what it sounds like.

I also found the Army will give me a little bit of traveling pay. That sure will help me out.

Well honey I've only got 2 more days before I graduate and 45 more days until I'll be home. I'm counting the days as they pass so slowly.

...I tried to call you tonight but they wouldn't let anybody use the phones tonight.   The D.I. said we were all confined to the company area because we were going to have a shakedown inspection. That's where they come through your barracks and confiscate anything that you are not supposed to have.

Have you thought about any new names yet? Have you decided how you are going to tell your mom about our big surprise?

Today we got some more shots and my arm is killing me.

Depending on how my next unit works for haircuts I might be able to come home with <u>long</u> hair. Pretty good huh?

...Well dear it's time to close once more so please remember not to write until I get my new address and send it to you.

I'll try to call before I leave here somehow. I love you with my heart <u>more</u> than you'll ever know.

With love in every stroke of my pen,

Jim   P.S. 45 more days!

Fort Polk
aka
'Tigerland'

Louisiana

November 5, 1966

to

December 17, 1966

Co. C 6th Bn 3rd Bde

November 5, 1966

Dearest Darling,

I just arrived in Louisiana. I can't stand it. It's so filthy and slummy looking. The people live in barns. They have no sense of personal hygiene what-so-ever. You just wouldn't believe some of the dirty, broken down, old houses I've seen people living in. This isn't the reason I wrote you. I wrote to tell you how much I love you and miss you.

Honey I know I've said it before but I never thought it could possibly be this bad. I'm so far away from you and it seems like I haven't seen you for a year and never will again...

...I've found out a way for me to come home but it costs like hell. Even if I don't make it on the 17th of Dec. its still going to cost plenty. Over $200.00 round trip. Honey we can't afford it! What am I going to do? I want to see you so bad but I know we can't afford that kind of money. I have 34 dollars and I get paid on the 1st of Dec. $45 or $50 dollars.

Have you gotten your allotment check yet? If not here is an address for you to write to....it must be in your own handwriting not typed. One of those 'Dear Sir' type of letter. If you already got the check hang on to the address anyway. They might goof up again.

My new address is:
PVT James D. Piper
US 56822929
Co.C 6th Bn 3rd Bde
Ft. Polk, Louisiana 71459
That's all that's necessary (except a letter from you).

Honey I've been so darn depressed all day today. Every time I think about how far away I am from you I get all choked up. I can't even write straight just by telling you about it.

This is going to be twice as hard as basic and its 9 weeks long, although we do get Christmas off. If I can get home.

Oh yeah! If by some miracle you come across some money fast , Ill tell you how to get me home. First you call the airport...I don't want you to suffer trying to get me home by working yourself to death or going into debt! If you want to you can sell my drums cheap...I just want to see you at any cost even if it means my drums. I can't play them now anyway.

...I'm miserably sick. I can't sleep and I've been worrying about getting home to you. My cold is worse.

...sweetheart I love you more now than ever before and more tomorrow than today. I just keep thinking about you and all the wonderful things we have shared together and will share in the future. Right now I'm going to start crying, but I don't dare infront of everyone here. Every time someone here mentions going home to his wife I get tears in my eyes. I love you darling, please don't leave me. I'm glad I'm not talking to you right now, it would be a total waste of money because my throat is all clogged up.

Darling I've got to close. Write soon.

My love forever and ever.

Jim

November 6, 1966

Hi Honey,

...I'm feeling a little better today and I'm not as depressed as I was earlier. I'm still not sure how in the hell I'll be able to come home. I'll make it somehow.

Well we start training on Nov. 7 and it's going to be really rough. I hope I can make it alright. Do you remember the Physical Training test I took at basic? Well I found out that I got 441 points last time. This A.I.T. is so hard we have to take 4 of those tests, 2 bivouacs, we have to qualify with the M-14 automatic rifle, M-16 Rifle, 45 caliber pistol, M-17 grenade launcher and the rocket launcher, 40 caliber and 50 caliber machine guns.

We have an inspection by the company Commander every day. I'm not a squad leader here so I can't get away with anything.

...I was just talking to some guys who signed up for the Army and they said they wanted to go into administration and Missiles and they were put in the infantry with me. So I know that the Army doesn't give you what you want. Even the guys at Ft. Lewis that I went through Basic with, 95% of them didn't get what they wanted.

The only ones that got what they wanted were Airborne and Infantry and one is just as bad as the other.

There were a few exceptions like Ken Old Coyote he got Administration but his best buddy wanted Chaplin's assistant and he went straight to Germany...I just hope I'm going to Germany after this training.

When I wrote that letter last night I thought I was losing my mind. I couldn't believe I was so far away from home and not able to see you. When I said I was miserable I meant it...Darling I hate this Army and I want to come home.

I think it's time that I close, so write back soon and often.

My love, Jim

Picture taken October 1966 (Developed December 1966.)
Jim Piper, Ken Old Coyote, and KPA

November 7, 1966

My Darling Wife,

    ...I don't want you to get upset or worried but I know for sure that I will be going to Viet Nam. I found out today during a talk with the company Commander and the Post Chaplin. I was sitting in class and the Brigade Commander had a record player and he played some Vietnamese music on it. When it was finished he told us that we would all get a chance to hear it in person.

    I'll get a Christmas leave on December 17 and then finish A.I.T. when I return. After that I'll get another 14 day leave then report to Oakland Amy Terminal or Ft Dix, New Jersey for Overseas Placement and shots...Honey I don't want to go to Viet Nam. I want to come home...

        All my love and more,
            Your hubby,

November 7, 1966:

> *Secretary of Defense Robert S. McNamara faced a storm of student protestors when he visited Harvard University to address a small group of students. When he left the dormitory, about 100 demonstrators shouted at him and when he attempted to leave demonstrators crowded around his automobile so that it could not move. Police intervened and escorted McNamara from the campus.*

> *Documents were released regarding the Viet Cong Irregular Strength, stating "additional evidence indicates that VC irregular strength is at least 250,000, double present figure; also relative numbers of guerrillas, militia and secret guerrillas have been*

misestimated by MACV (military assistance command, Vietnam."

November 9, 1966

Hi Darling,

...Please don't worry too much about those letters I wrote before because most of it was bullshit that I just found out about. The Drill Sergeants are trying to scare you into working harder so we can learn to save our lives if we are called to serve in Viet Nam which is possible but not always true.

The only thing I am still very worried about is getting home for Christmas. But I still have plenty of time to cross that bridge. Although it doesn't hurt to think about it.

You should have seen what happened today. A guy in the first platoon had $250.00 stolen from him and they caught the guy that did it. They took him into custody and he will be court marshaled and sentenced to 5 years in prison then he has to do 2 years of service after that. That's pretty rough but it serves him right. I'm putting the rest of my money in the company safe until I desperately need it. I can't afford to let what little I have get stolen.

...Only 38 more days before I can come home...
...Lights out will write more tomorrow.
Love,
        Jim

Hi again honey,

Most of my letters will probably be broken up like this for the first 2 weeks here because of our review classes at night. ...Tomorrow is a holiday (Armistice Day) so I think I'll be able to write another letter.

...I will be home but I may not make it in time for the Christmas party which I'm looking forward to going to. I will be home within 44 hours of midnight the 16th. That means no later than 8 PM on the 18th. That's our anniversary and I want to be home for that because it will be a whole 6 months we've been married and only lived together for 2. Just wait until 4:00 PM August 29, 1968. That's the exact date and time that I get out. Boy what a celebration that is going to be. I hope our daughters won't be old enough to see their father drunk and sick. I wouldn't want them to blackmail me someday when they get older.

I still like the name of Shawna Marie, but do you have as good a name for a twin if we have a set? Well at least one child has a name. What if it's a boy? He'd hate us if we named him Shawna Marie.

Darling its time for me to close for now so please write soon.

My love everlasting,

Jim

P.S. This letter was written by a genuine Tiger Cub in Tigerland, Ft. Polk.

Note:
Fort Polk was known as 'Tigerland' the training grounds for infantrymen for Vietnam.

November 11, 1966

Hi Sweetheart,

...Today is a holiday so I thought I would get a nice long letter off to you. I never can tell when my next few minutes of free time will be.

I went to the P.X. and bought you a birthday card. I hope you won't feel hurt honey, but I just couldn't buy you anything or pay for the mailing of it besides. I'll make up for it though. I don't want you to get me anything for Christmas understand?! Its going to be a mighty slim Christmas this year but I think we both understand the situation now. When I finally get out of this Army we'll have a honeymoon and Christmas all rolled into one. Maybe even a small party.

I'll tell you what we did last week.

Sunday was orientation day. It's a lot like your first day of school where the teacher tells you all the school rules etc. It was about ½ mile away and we had to run all the way to it. Afterwards we ran back and had lunch. Then we ran about 1 ½ miles to the Magnolia Theater where the Brigade Commander talked to us...then we ran back from that.

Monday I had it fairly easy. All I did was run to the Quarter Masters Supply and picked up about 45 pounds of equipment and ran back. About 3 ½ miles altogether.

Tuesday we had a class on land mine warfare for 8 whole hours. Ran to and from, 2 miles.

Wednesday we had a radio and wireless communication class for 8 hours. Ran to and from 2 ½ miles.

Thursday we ran 2 ½ miles to and from a Compass and Map reading class. 8 whole hours.

We have to run a mile everyday before breakfast, plus running to and from every (classroom type) class we have.

...I guess you are wondering why I am writing so often and every chance I get. Well, its because I'm so lonely I can't stand it. Then when I write I feel better and closer to home. Today is Friday and I'm hoping for a better tomorrow.

...Tomorrow I have to get up at 3:30 AM so we can have a fire power demonstration at 6:00 AM. That's where we get to see all the types of weapons fired and what kind of damage they do.

...I was just laying here on my bed looking at your picture and our wedding picture. Do you know I've had more comments on what a boss looking wife I have that it sure makes me proud and homesick.

..I still don't know if you've received your allotment check yet. Did you write to that place that I gave you the address for? If not, do it as soon as possible if you don't have your allotment yet.

...Honey...I could never explain the need I have for you or the unending love which is rapidly growing every minute and every second that we are apart.

...Honey I have to go to my initiation as a Tiger Cub. I'll be back when I'm finished.

Guess what? I was blindfolded and taken to the Tiger Den by a couple of the Squad Leaders. The Tiger Den is a beer hall and you should have seen what I had to do. They took the blindfold off and made me get on the table on my hands and knees. Then they placed a saucer of beer on the table and told me to lap it up like a cat or a tiger. Then I had to roar like a tiger. Well now I'm a full-fledged Tiger and can go to the Tiger Den whenever I want...After the initiation guys were buyng me beer and congratulating me. After a couple of beers I got to play the drums. It sure brings back memories. I haven't forgotten as much as I thought I did. But I still want you to sell my drums if you can. Besides it will be one less bill you have to worry about.

...I sure feel safer with my money in the safe. They had another theft today of $56.00. I'm only keeping $3.00 with me for emergencies. I've tried to stop smoking and I think I'm progressing quite well. I've cut down considerably so maybe I won't have to quit. It's the only enjoyment I get out of the Army, besides free time to write to you.

Oh, before I forget, we had a lightning and thunder storm today. It poured almost all day long and its nothing but mud all around us.

Well this is goodnight darling.

I'll be writing again soon I hope.

All my love forever,

Jim

November 14, 1966: intelligence reported that the GVN planned to undertake a massive psychological warfare operation commencing in January 1967 to encourage defection among the middle-level Viet Cong cadre. For propaganda purposes, previous defectors from the Viet Cong were to be used in the program.

November 13, 1966

Hi Darling,

...Guess what? I only have 35 more days before I come home. That's 4 days longer than a month and I'm looking forward to coming home so I can once again hold you in my arms...from the 17th of December to the 2nd of Jan I can be a civilian again for 15 days.

...I wish you could have been at graduation with me. After graduation all the parents and wives came to our company area and were served donuts and coffee and escorted around to see what the barracks looked like...everyone was sitting in cars, hugging and kissing and just crying. I felt like a lost sheep...I went for a walk to the dayroom and stayed there until it was time to catch my plane.

...Boy the weather here is really crazy. When I get up in the morning about 4:30 A.M. its warm enough to go swimming. Then about 7:00 to 10:00 A.M. it gets real cold. Its almost 50 degrees or lower. Then around 10:30 A.M. to 3:00 P.M. its so hot you can't stand it. The humidity is so bad you can't breath.

...I was told by the C.O. this type of Infantry training is harder than any Marine training in the United States. Most of these guys think that we can take on anything on two legs. Many of them specialize in Marines. Not me. I'm still the chicken hearted type and will probably stay that way except that I can defend myself in any situation and I'm a little bit stronger than before.

By the way, how is Oakland? Are they still having those riots?

...

All my love forever,

Jim

Note:

On the heels of the August 11, 1965 Watts Riots in Southern California, urban riots continued into 1966, occurring in 20 cities, including San Francisco, Oakland, Cleveland, Chicago, Omaha, the underlying cause of the riots were the social conditions of the areas. In Oakland, the newly formed Black Panther Party, founded by activists Huey P. Newton and Bobby Seale, employed armed members -- "Panthers" -- to shadow police officers who, they believed, unfairly targeted blacks. In San Francisco the Compton Riot made headlines.

November 15, 1966

Hi Sweetie,

...I was so happy to get your letter and especially the one with the time schedule for the flight...all I need now is some information on how to confirm it.

...Today I got to fire the M79 anti-tank weapon. They had a bunch of target tanks on the range and I blew one up. The M79 is a rocket launcher and it shoots a rocket that weighs 9 lbs...Then I got to fire a light anti-tank weapon. It's called the law missile and it costs $41.00 and can only be fired once then thrown away. It's the same thing as the M79 only smaller and more accurate. I blew up another tank with it.

Right now it's 3:00 A.M. and I'm on fire watch. We have to get up at 3:45 today so I volunteered so I could get the letter written.

...

Love,

Jim

P.S. Thank you so much for making the reservation for me.

I love you.

Jim

***

November 15, 1966:

➤ Chairman of the Joint Chiefs of Staff, General Earle Wheeler, addressed a gathering at Brown University and approximately 60 students walk out to protest his defense of U.S. involvement in Vietnam. Some students that remained shouted and heckled Wheeler while others attempted to storm the stage. Outside over 100 students continued the protest.

> *Secretary Rusk addressed the annual meeting of the Association of State Colleges and National Association of State Universities and Land Grant Colleges regarding "aggression in South Viet-Nam" finishing his speech with:*

"Our commitments are the backbone of world peace. It is essential that neither our adversaries nor our friends ever doubt that we will do what we say we will do. Otherwise, the result is very likely to be a great catastrophe.

In his last public utterance President Kennedy reviewed what the United States had done to preserve freedom and peace since the Second World War, and our defensive commitments, including our support of South Viet-Nam. He said: 'We are still the keystone in the arch of freedom and I think we will continue to do as we have done in the past, our duty…'"

November 17, 1966

...Hey you should hear some of the crazy things we say when we are marching. Here are a few of the ones we sing or say:

I've got a girl with a '32 Ford
She likes to screw on the running board
Sound off 1-2
Sound off 3-4
Cadence count 1-2-3-4, 1-2, 3-4.

There's a lot more of them but I don't want to waste the paper on them.

Tomorrow after my test the Sergeant told me that he would take me to the South Fort with him so I can confirm the reservations. After that I'll be all set except for coming home. For that I'll have to wait 28 more days. Just 4 short weeks, isn't that great?

Well dear its time to go so I'll write again soon. Don't worry because I'll make that flight on time.

My love forever,
Jim.

November 18, 1966:

➢ *Vietcong attacked the USARV (U.S. Army, Vietnam) Long Binh ammunition dump in Bien Hoa Province destroying 1,265 105-mm artillery rounds.*

➢ *The US stated that aid programs undertaken by the USSR and Communist China estimated that "military aid amounting to about $250 million and economic aid amounting to $150 million was delivered in 1965. The amount of aid increased in 1966, and recent trends indicate that it will continue to increase in 1967."*

November 21, 1966

Dearest 19 year old wife,

Today is your birthday...do you know that I have exactly 646 hours 42 minutes from now until our first kiss after almost 4 months...I've got 39,802 minutes or 2,288,120 seconds until I finally step off the plane in San Francisco and can once again hold you in my arms.

...Happy Birthday and have a wonderful Thanksgiving and don't eat too much.

My ultra expressed love,

Jim

November 24, 1966

Hi Sweetie,

Gee it was wonderful to hear your soft soothing voice again...sometimes I can't remember what you sound like but every time I call I still recognize the voice of my darling wife.

I'm so glad you got the allotment check finally. Now maybe it will start coming in regularly and you can pay off some of those bills.

...Only 23 more days until they won't be so long and lonely anymore. Boy am I looking forward to that first night. I imagine that you are kind of anxious too.

...Hey have you started writing out Christmas cards yet? I'll bet you're going to have a lot of fun with that, ha, ha. I remember how much you loved to write out those thank you notes after we were married. Do me a big favor and have them all done before I get home. I'm not trying to get out of it or anything but I've got to make up for lost time and can't afford to lose too much in writing cards. Right?!

...Darling I know this sounds a little raw at times but somehow I just can't help it. You are the only one I love...Honey I'm so tired of being alone at night that sometimes I dream of all the wonderful, thrilling affairs we have had together. Like the first night of our marriage. I can remember all the beautiful things we said to each other and how well we meant them.

I also remember some of the funny things that happened like the time we played strip poker and I lost and had to dress up in your clothes and you put two peaches in your bra and I couldn't get it off so you smashed one of the peaches.

...Darling your enchanting ways of making love to me have kept my love from ever dying and will keep it strong as the years go by. Your gentleness is not measured in just mere words...Honey I am so fully and deeply content with our love.

...Just think of all the nights we will have together after I get out of this damn Army. After my leave I'll only have 20 months to go before I get out and that will be at 4:00 P.M. August 29, 1968. Hooray. I've already done 1/8 of my Army service, only 7/8 of it to go. After my leave I'll have 1/6 of it done and will only have 5/6 to go. It sounds kind of good when I put it in fractions.

Darling its time for me to close now. Take good care of yourself for me while I'm away.

My love forever and ever,

Jim

November 24, 1966: the battle of Attleboro ended. The operation involved a total of 22,000 allied troops, 12,000 tons of tactical air support, 35,000 artillery rounds and 11 B-52 strikes. 1,106 VC killed, 44 captured. Friendly losses, 155 KIA and 494 WIA.

November 26, 1966

Dearest honeybunch,

...I really don't know if I'm going to Vietnam or not. Around February the President said he was going to send 40,000 to Korea and 56,000 to Germany all from infantry, so keep your pretty little fingers crossed. That doesn't mean that I'll be chosen to go to either of those places but at least it's something to hope for.

...Guess what? You will start receiving a savings bond every month and if you want to cash it to pay bills you can. The Company Commander wanted 100% participation so I had to get one. Besides if I go to Vietnam or some other Combat zone I will be getting combat pay which is about $55.00 more so I will be making $169.80 a month.

...Love you lots

Jim

November 29, 1966

Hi Sweetheart,

Sorry about being late again but I just can't seem to find the time to write much this week…we have to get haircuts again I'll let you know a little later how it turned out…my haircut isn't too bad, at least they let me keep the top. Its not much but at least its hair. I don't have enough to run a comb through yet but I might have some by Christmas.

Honey I am getting so excited about going home that I want to start packing now.

Can you think of any guys at home that would be willing to join the Army? For every guy that I get to join the Army I get a 5 day leave. Or I can have the time knocked off my term of service…I wouldn't recommend the Army to any friends.

Honey the lights just went out and I'm trying to write by the light of a lighter.

With all my everlasting love and deep affection,
Jim.
P.S. I love you.

November 30, 1966: the South Vietnamese Constituent Assembly met in Saigon and began drawing up draft articles for a new constitution.

Chapter Four

DECEMBER 1966

"I love you so much and miss you so much...I almost cry
because I know how much you mean to me."

December 2, 1966: in a memorandum addressed to:
Chief, Indochina Division,
Information stated that the "so-called 'Main Force Support
Personnel' listed in MACV's OB on the Viet Cong are carried at a
strength far below their actual numbers."

Personnel

	1965	1966
Total personnel estimate	*17,533*	*100,000 +- 1000*
COSVN	*3,970*	
Region Hqs.	*2,910*	
Province Hqs	*800*	*11,000*
Sappers (Com. Engineers)	*750*	*thousands*
Intel/Recon	*660*	*thousands*
Guard	*410*	*thousands*
Production	*3,160*	*unclear amount*
Transport Corridor		
Opns and Commo/Liason	*5,893*	*considerably more*

No category for 'Assault Youth' which carried supplies, policed
battlefields and performed other functions; many armed.

Unofficially the Army Assistant Chief of Staff for Intelligence
(ACSI) put the number of the 'Main Force Support Personnel' at
40-50,000. ACSI added an additional 26,400 support soldiers,
transport units, communication personnel and boat crews,
estimating the probable strength of the Main Force Support
Personnel as high as 100,000.

December 2, 1966: Joint Chief of Staff asked direct substitution
of units to provide "balanced forces."

December 3, 1966

...we had a "flash inspection" at 10:30 P.M. The inspection was on all the foot lockers to see if anyone had candy or food that was going to be left behind next week. The only reason they don't want food left in them is so the cockroaches won't walk away with the barracks.

Thank you sweetheart for the tickets. I finally got a chance to go to the brigade Mail room and pick them up. Boy I sure am glad I've got my tickets because everybody who doesn't have them by now is up a creek without a paddle. They can't get any reservations to go anywhere on the West coast. I sure was lucky.

...When I get off that plane I'm going to run through the gate, up the stairs, down the ramp, and straight to you without even looking around to see who I knocked down. Then I'm going to take you in my arms and kiss you and kiss you and kiss you until I have to come up for air. After that I'll see if my mom and dad are around and go say hi to them.

...Well tomorrow we go on Bivouac and get back Thursday around 8:00 P.M. After that I only have 8 days to go. It sure is getting close now.

...Darling I hate to end each letter I write to you but there just isn't enough time in my training day to write as long a letter as I would like to.

I love you so much and miss you so much that with the Christmas leave coming up I almost cry because I know how much you mean to me.

Every ounce of my love,
Jim

···

December 4, 1966: a Viet Cong unit penetrated a 13-mile defense perimeter around Saigon's Tan Son Nhut airport shelling the field for over four hours. The attackers, receiving 18 casualties, were driven off by South Vietnamese and U.S. Security guards. The attackers returned the same night and received 11 more casualties before being driven off again.

December 8, 1966

Hi Sweetheart,

Well I'm back from Bivouac. I got to come back earlier than the other guys because I'm on K.P. tomorrow and all the K.P.s have to fix breakfast and take it out to the rest of the company. I sure am glad because it started raining right before I left our camp site. The other guys have to sleep out in the rain while I sleep in a nice warm barracks.

...I only have 7 more days to go before I can hold you again. It sure is going by fast.

...Honey I'm going to have to close now so I can get some sleep. 2:30 A.M. comes awfully early around here.

Remember that I love you deeply and will be home soon to prove it.

All my love,
Jim

December 8, 1966: the International Red Cross announced in Geneva that North Vietnam had rejected a proposal by President Johnson for a resolution of the prisoner of war situation. He had proposed a joint discussion of fair treatment and possible exchange of war captives held by both sides. The International Red Cross submitted the proposal to North Vietnamese officials in July after Johnson first broached the plan on July 20 at a news conference.

Note: No solution was reached on the issue until the Paris Peace Accords were signed in January 1973. By the terms of the accords, all U.S. prisoners were to be released by the following March.

December 9, 1966: a memo from Secretary of Defense to Chairman Joint Chiefs of Staff, approved direct substitution within 470,000 man ceiling.

December 11, 1966

Hi Darling,

I have some time to write you now so I thought it was about time. I imagine you agree don't you?

Well I thought I might be forgiven when I tell you I only have 6 days to go before I'm home. Wow it is close!

Tonight I got to play the drums again. I'll tell you how it all came about. I was in the barracks getting ready for the inspection tonight and missed dinner. So I got hungry and went to the snack bar with a couple of the guys. Well after I devoured a couple of hot dogs and french fries, one of my buddies came running in and asked me if I played the drums. He said, "I thought you did. Come on over to the Service Club, they need a drummer." Well I got to play a set exactly like my set except the floor tom was a little smaller than mine.

...I'll be in San Francisco at 7:13 P.M. on Saturday so please don't be late; as if you really would be.

I'm getting so excited that the guys around here in the barracks think I'm losing my marbles. I've really been in a good mood and have been laughing and joking with them and I never did before as much as now.

There is one guy here from Tennessee that is a real nut. Yesterday we were on a force march back from one of the squad tactics ranges and he got mad at the squad leader for marching too fast and the guys with short legs couldn't keep up.

Well later we were walking to the supply room and he turned to me and said, "Boy am I glad that march is over, I couldn't go much further at that pace."

I said, "That squad leader thinks hes part giraffe with those long legs of his." And he said, "I know, and I called that son of a bitch everything but a white person and he still wouldn't slow down." The way he said it was so funny at the time I laughed until I cried and my sides and stomach ached.

Well sweetie I'll have to close for now. I probably won't write any more because I will be home before the letter gets there.

Remember I love you darling and will prove it when I once again can hold you in my arms.

My lasting love,
Forever,
Jim

ONLY 6 DAYS LEFT

Christmas Leave
Micki's memories

"When my Jim arrived in SFO, I was dressed in a silver cocktail dress (looking pretty good) because we were headed to the Hawaiian clubs' Christmas party right from the airport. When he saw me, he had a big grin on his face and he came running. It was just like it was in the movies. We saw each other and ran as fast as we could – hugging, kissing, more hugging, more kissing.

We arrived at the party being held at the Alameda Hotel in Alameda- I still remember, what a feeling it was when Jim (in his full dress uniform) and I walked in...everyone started clapping for him. I was so proud of him. So proud to be his wife."

···

"We spent the first evening together, alone, in his parents' home. They had left so we could be together. But it wasn't as romantic as we had hoped.

When we were in the kitchen I saw a mouse. I jumped on the portable dishwasher, the kind you had to pull out and hook up to the kitchen sink, and screamed. I wouldn't get down until Jim found the mouse and killed it.

Looking back its really funny; me sitting on the dishwasher, Jim running around the kitchen with a broom smacking at the little mouse. It's a fun memory. I'll never forget that night."

···

"The first week of January Jim had to report back to the Oakland Army Base. It was at this time his orders were for

Vietnam. He was there for three days in lock down and then shipped out to Vietnam.

During those three days I made a call to the base, though I thought it was a futile attempt, but a guy answered the phone so I asked to talk to a Jim Piper. He yelled "Is there a Private Piper here?" There was an answer, "Yes sir."

That was the last time I got to talk to him, the last time I heard his voice.

I kept thinking how lucky I was to hear him one last time."

James Dennis Piper 1965

Wedding Day June 18, 1966

June 18, 1966

Senior Prom 1965 San Lorenzo High School (Jim's H.S.)

Sunset High School 1965 Senior Prom (Micki's H.S.)

Hi Darling.

I love you. Here I am writing you a letter right after getting in from Drills. I've still got my helmet on.

Some of those streaks are from the Flash attachment on the camera.

Love you much. Me.

Intelligence Report

DIRECTORATE OF
INTELLIGENCE

The Situation in South Vietnam
(Weekly)

30 January 1967
No. 0335/67

Example of a cover sheet for a declassified CIA document
archived in the Lyndon Baines Johnson library.

1.3(a)(4)

1.3(a)(4)

1.3(a)(4)

Secret

More often than not, the declassified documents were less than revealing.

December 13 & 14, 1966: US bombing raids damaged Chinese and Soviet embassies in North Vietnam.

...

December 19, 1966: US Government intelligence addressed a New York Times article written December 18, 1966 claiming the number of VC defections and desertions were rising implying that VC are experiencing serious morale problems. The US stated that the defection numbers may be correct but maintained that deserters who do not defect far outnumber those who do.

...

December 21, 1966: CIA intercepted an intelligence cable regarding alleged plans by retired Major General Tran Van Don, Nationalist Party member Xuan Tung and former Dai Viet Luong Quoc Xung to overthrow the South Vietnamese government and to assassinate Prime Minister Nguyen Cao Ky.

...

December 23, 1966: Francis Cardinal Spellman, the Roman Catholic Archbishop of New York and Military Vicar of the U.S. armed forces for Roman Catholics, delivered an address at mass in Saigon stating that the Vietnamese conflict was "a war for civilization—certainly it is not a war of our seeking. It is a war thrust upon us—we cannot yield to tyranny." Anything "less than victory is inconceivable."

December 25, 1966: assistant managing editor of the New York Times, Harrison Salisbury, filed a report from Hanoi reporting the damage to civilian areas in North Vietnam by a U.S. Bombing Campaign. Salisbury stated that Nam Dinh, a city about 50 miles southeast of Hanoi, was bombed repeatedly by U.S. planes starting on June 28, 1965. Pentagon officials contended that he was exaggerating the damage to civilian areas.

December 26, 1966:

> ➤ *U.S. Defense Department conceded that American pilots had bombed North Vietnamese civilians accidentally during missions against military targets. The spokesman restated administration policy that air raids were confined to military targets but added, "It is sometimes impossible to avoid all damage to civilian areas."*

> ➤ *Three days after his address to US troops during mass at Saigon, Francis Cardinal Spellman told U.S. soldiers that they were in Vietnam for the "defense, protection, and salvation not only of our country, but... of civilization itself." The next day, Vatican sources expressed displeasure with Spellman's statements in Vietnam. One source said, "The Cardinal did not speak for the Pope or the Church." The Pope had previously called for negotiations and an end to the war in Vietnam.*

December 27, 1966:

- ➤ *The Christmas truce in Vietnam ended in the early morning hours when the 22nd NVA moved into position around LZ Bird in the Kim Son Valley attacking with a barrage of small arms and mortar fire.*

- ➤ *A United States and South Vietnamese joint-service operation took place against one of the best-fortified Viet Cong strongholds, located in the U Minh Forest in the Mekong Delta, 125 miles southwest of Saigon. U.S. warplanes dropped bombs and napalm on the forest followed by an attack on Viet Cong Positions in the forest by 6,000 South Vietnamese troops.*

Dec 29, 1966:

- ➤ *Assistant Secretary of Defense, Arthur Sylvester, admitted that the North Vietnamese city of Nam Dinh had been hit by U.S. planes 64 times since mid-1965. He stated the air strikes were directed only against military targets: railroad yards, a warehouse, petroleum storage depots, and a thermal power plant. He criticized New York Times correspondent Harrison Salisbury's reports on results of those air raids as "misstatements of fact."*

- ➤ *Student body Presidents' from 100 U.S. colleges and Universities signed an open letter to President Lyndon B. Johnson expressing anxiety and doubt over the involvement of the United States in Vietnam, further stating that many youths might prefer prison over participation in the war. There was no response from the President.*

> CIA Intelligence information reported an account of North Vietnamese criticism of Soviet motives for its support of North Vietnam and the Viet Cong in their war efforts.

December 30 1966: news sources reported that Chairman Mendel Rivers of the House Armed Services Committee called upon the U.S. to "flatten Hanoi if necessary and let the world opinion go fly a kite."

December 31, 1966:

> *Ambassador Lodge, in his New Year's Eve statement, predicted that "allied forces will make sensational military gains in 1967" and "the war would end in an eventual fadeout once the allied pacification effort made enough progress to convince Hanoi that the jig was up."*

> *The New York Day News headlines read "U.S. Expects to Crush Main Red Force in '67."*

> *Report stated that the US combat death toll had reached 5,008 KIA and 30,093 WIA.*

> *Pentagon Reports estimated the cost of the 'conflict' amounted to 9.1 billion in '66. The estimate was 19.7 billion for '67 and for '68 "if forces and rates of operations are stabilized" the estimated cost would be "about 24 billion."*

Chapter Five

JANUARY 1967

"My wife and children will <u>never</u> see Communism or its principles."

After an all-too brief leave, Jim Piper shipped back to Ft. Polk, aka Tigerland, Louisiana, to continue his AIT training (Advanced Individual Training) January 1, 1967.

January 1, 1967: US troops in South Vietnam were at 385,000.

Early January: Thailand announced they were dispatching 1000 troops to South Vietnam, becoming part of an allied force joining approximately 45,000 South Vietnamese and 7000 Australians.

January 2, 1967

Hi Sweetheart,

I sure am sorry I had to leave, I didn't realize how homesick I was until I got on the plane from Dallas to Ft. Polk. That is when I noticed you were so far away from me and I finally broke down. I couldn't hold it any longer. Honey I love you so much I wish to hell I was never drafted. Although being drafted has made me realize how much we love each other and if I can't tell you in a letter, you should know it by now.

...Guess what? I went to the orderly room last night to sign in and I saved one day of my leave so I'll have one day extra to spend with you next time. Also by signing in early I pulled K.P. in the morning for the fourth time. But I don't mind since it means I get to spend an extra day with you.

By the way I know this is illegal but I'm sending you some money in this letter because I know you are broke. I should have gave you some money before I left because the car is almost out of gas. I hope you get this letter before it does.

...There's only one good thing about returning to this place and that is that after "Peason Ridge" I'll only have one week before I come home again and I'm already looking forward to it.

Honey you just can't imagine how much I enjoyed my Christmas at home with you...

Darling I'm going to have to close for now because I have a lot of unpacking to do before I go to bed.

Write as soon as you can. I love you very much and miss you terribly.

All my love,
            Jim

Note: Peason Ridge is located north of Ft Polk consisting of 33,011 acres of non-contiguous Army training area, containing hill terrain, creeks, forest and open land.

*January 2, 1967: U.S. Air Force F-4 Phantom jets downed seven MiG-21s over North Vietnam. During this air battle Col. Robin Olds shot down one of the MiGs, becoming the first and only U.S. Air Force 'ace' with victories in **both** WWII and Vietnam.*

January 3, 1967

Hi Honey,

I just got in from a night patrol and cleaned my rifle and turned it in then made my bed and polished my boots and still have time to write you a long letter before turning in for the night.

I took another picture and I sure am enjoying having that camera. The guys in the picture with me are Willie Smith from New York and my high school buddy Steve Anderson who lives over on Via Grenada.

The three of us are inseparable during training and even on the week-ends...If my and Steve's face looks dirty its because when we went out on patrol we had to put on camouflage paint to take the shine off our faces at night. Willie told us to go wash it off that he was lucky and his didn't show. He's really a character.

It sure is cold here right now. I wish you were here to keep me warm, but my bed isn't even big enough for myself so I guess I'll just have to suffer for two or three more weeks until

I can come home again. I sure have had a hard time trying to sleep without you here. I keep waking up at night and want to cuddle up to you but you're not there and then I start thinking about you and how much I miss you and love you...

Next week we will go up to Peason Ridge for 5 days so I won't be able to write again just like bivouac. I just hope it doesn't rain but with my kind of luck I know it will. Please pray for sunshine and 90 degree weather next week.

Tomorrow we get to fire the 50 caliber machine gun, then 1 hour of physical training, 1 hour of marching, and I think I get off early for a change.

Friday we have escape and evasion and we won't get in until 12:30 that night. We also have PT test that day. I'll bet I'm really out of shape after being home for Christmas and with my cold being worse I'll never do as well as my last couple of times.

Well darling I just had an offer from one of the guys to take my fireguard shift for me because I need some rest to get rid of my cold I'm going to take advantage of it.

I love you so much...
All my love forever,
Your Hubby,
Jim

""

January 3, 1967: the 26th ROK Regiment (Tiger Division) initiated MAENG HO 8, a 60 day search and destroy operation in Binh Dinh and Phu Yen Provinces. At the conclusion on March 6, 1967, the enemy losses were 211 killed, 375 POWs, 699 detained, 145 individual weapons and 34 crew-served weapons. Friendly losses were 7 KIAs and 19 WIAs.

January 4, 1967

Dearest Darling,

...I got paid today and pulled $29.00 this month with $25 dollars for partial pay and your allotment. I was surprised that I got that much.

Next month you will be getting the $25 savings bond along with your allotment.

Did you get your allotment for this month yet?

I got a hair cut today but it wasn't too bad...They call it "White Walls" because they cut the edges real short and leave the top long. At least I didn't have to get it all cut off like usual.

...Guess what I just heard? Everyone that is going to Viet Nam if they do will only be for 9 months instead of 12 months. But as far as I know for sure its just a rumor...I still haven't received my orders yet so don't worry. I still don't think I'm going but I'm not going to get my hopes up too high...

...Time to sign out tonight. I love you more than ever before.

                    Jim

January 4, 1967: USN A-4 and F-4 aircraft were downed by enemy ground fire over North Vietnam. The crews were rescued.

January 5, 1967

Hi Darling,

Here it is the 5th day of January and I've written you three letters and this one makes the fourth. Now you know that I miss you and love you so much. I've written every day so far and I'll keep pushing the pen until Sunday because that's when I go to Peason Ridge. I won't be able to write you next week and that is going to break my perfect record.

...Honey do you have any nylons with runs in them that you are going to throw out? Well don't throw them out because they are real good for spit shining shoes. Please send me a couple if you have them. They work great.

Guess what I'm going to do if I go overseas? I'm going to ask for 2 extra weeks on my next leave so I can spend a month with you. I'm pretty sure I can get it.

...Have you seen any houses you would like to have in San Lorenzo ? I've been thinking about getting a house and fixing it all up and moving in and I can't wait. I'm looking forward to that almost as much as getting out of here.

Well honey I have to polish my boots before I start on the barracks so I'll have to close for now. Don't forget to write next week, even if I can't answer them right away.

...My love forever & ever,

Jim

January 5, 1967:

> ➢ *Amphibious operations in Kien Hoa Province in the Mekong Delta 62 miles south of Saigon were conducted by 1st Battalion, 9th U.S. Marines and South Vietnamese Marine Brigade Force Bravo.*

> ➢ *Operation Niagara Falls, a three day deception operation began in the Cau Dinh jungle of Binh Duong Province, designed to place combat elements in position before striking the main blow.*

> ➢ *Operation Seine, a 9-day search & destroy mission in Quang Ngai Provinc was launched. Upon completion of the operation January 14 the total enemy losses were 140 killed, 71 detained, 15 ralliers and four individual weapons. Friendly losses were 37 killed and 56 wounded.*

January 6, 1967

Hi Sweetie,

Here I am again and I've got a lot to tell you about what happened to me today.

Tonight we had 'escape & evasion' from the enemy. The whole point of the training was to see if I could get through enemy lines back to friendly lines without getting captured.

Well, me, Willie and Steve and about four other guys were all together and we were doing real well by staying away from the enemy and getting back until we picked up a stranger along the way. We had already walked, crawled, and ran about 4 miles when this guy that escaped from the concentration camp decided to join up with us. We didn't mind because we were almost back to the friendly lines. While we were talking with him the enemy surrounded us and captured me & Willie and two others.

They made us walk with our hands above our heads and lay down in the dirt that way until a truck came to pick us up and take us to the concentration camp.

They through (throw) us on the truck we were taken to the camp and the treatment we got there I wouldn't want to go through again.

First I was taken off the truck and asked if I was going to cooperate and I didn't say anything, I just looked at him. He asked again and I still didn't answer. Then he tripped me and I fell to the ground where another guy took over and tried to get some information out of me by putting his elbow in my neck and choking me until I couldn't breath. I know this is just training but he didn't have to be that rough. But that's not all. I still wouldn't talk and he picked me up off the ground and stuck his thumbs in the base of my throat and I told him my name, rank, service number, and date of birth like I'm supposed to do. That's all the information I was allowed to give out if I was captured but he still wanted more.

He asked me how to spell it and I told him to go to hell and I hate your guts. Then he let me go and told me to go join a bunch of other prisoners doing exercises.

After the exercises I had a good opportunity to escape so I did and got back to friendly lines once again.

Right now its 1:30 AM and I'm beat. I still haven't taken a shower yet and I better pretty soon.

Today was Friday and I still didn't get a letter from you and I was expecting one so much.

...Honey I love you so much and miss you greatly. I hope my next leave is as pleasurable and relaxing as the last one. I also hope I get that extra two weeks if I go overseas.

Its about time for that shower because I can't stand myself anymore. Please write soon darling. I love you so much it hurts me to be away from you or not hear from you in a long while.

Your loving hubby,
Jim

January 6, 1967: USAF F-4 aircrafts downed two MIG-21's raising the downed MIG total to 36.

January 6 – 15, 1967: The only use of USMC ground forces in the Mekong Delta went ashore between the Ham Luong and Co Chien rivers in the Kien Hoa Province in Operation Song Than/Deckhouse V. It was the last SLF landing outside the boundaries of I Corps.

January 7, 1967

...I just finished packing my duffle bag to go to Peason Ridge tomorrow. I hope I have enough time to write you before I leave. I'll be back here by Friday around 12:00 noon. So I'll start my letter again. I might go to the Post Exchange and get some postcards and send them while I'm on Peason Ridge. It will be much easier than writing letters and I'll be able to write every day too...

Honey it felt so good talking to you today. It really built up my moral and determination to finish this training. Thank God its almost over with. I've been miserable here in Ft. Polk without you here with me. Even the short time we were married before I was drafted I didn't think it was going to hurt us as much as it does. Just keep thinking positive that I'll be back in 19 months for good and we can start thinking seriously about a selection of a home. I've got a couple of good ideas for interior and outside decorating. We sure are going to have a lot of fun fixing it up the way we will enjoy it.

...Some of the guys brought small portable record players and now we sit around and listen to some good music for a change. They have all kinds of albums like the Ventures, Mama's + Papa's, Dave Clark 5, and Gary Lewis and the Playboys...

Honey its time for me to close so I will be able to get a lot of sleep tonight before we go to Peason Ridge tomorrow.

I love you with all my heart,

Your loving true hubby,

Jim

•••

January 7, 1967: an enemy attack occurred on Camp Holloway Airfield 4km E of Pleiku City with a ground assault supported by mortar fire. Friendly losses were light casualties, light equipment and aircraft damage.

January 8, 1967

Hi Sweets,

This is my seventh letter and guess what? I won't be able to send those post cards anyway because they aren't going to have mail pick up out there unless its an emergency. I don't know why but that's what our Captain said a little while ago. We will be able to receive mail but not send out because of the type of training we're having we are supposed to be isolated without any type of communication or contact with civilization. The only thing they can do is bring in our mail from home because of some law by the government mail system.

You might have guessed that this will be the last letter until I get back from field. But you should receive this letter either Wednesday or Thursday so it won't be so bad if I get back on Friday. Also I can't put a picture in this letter because I am out of flashbulbs. The flashbulbs that the other guys got me were the wrong kind so I gave them to one of the guys in the barracks.

Most of the guys are just sitting around waiting to fall out for the next company formation. That's when we will be taking off and I hope I have time to finish this letter before we go.

Talking to you yesterday was so nice that it made me homesick all over again. You can't imagine what its like to be 2,200 miles from you and have to go through some of the bull they've been handing out here. Its like prison and everybody thinks you're a dumb convict and they put you in isolation so you can't see your loved ones. That's exactly what it feels like.

I just keep thinking about graduation and coming home again and it doesn't seem too bad.

Well darling, I better close and make sure I have all the proper clothing I need to keep warm and dry while I'm gone. I don't want to get any worse than I am now.

Remember I love you and please keep writing.

All my lasting love,   James

Jan 8 – 26: Approximately 16,000 U.S. soldiers join 14,000 South Vietnamese troops to mount Operation Cedar Falls; an operation designed to disrupt insurgent operations near Siagon. During the operation a massive tunnel complex was discovered and destroyed in the Iron Triangle: a 60 square mile area of jungle in the Thanh Dein Forest believed to contain communist camps and supply dumps. At the end of the operation approximately 711 enemies were reported killed and up to 488 captured. Allied losses reported approximately 83 killed, 345 wounded.

January 9, 1967: The Agency for International Development (AID) attempted to respond to reports in the American media of widespread corruption and commodities sold on the black market that had been sent to South Vietnam by the United States. In a report to the president, AID officials asserted, "No more than 5-6 percent of all economic assistance commodities delivered to Vietnam were stolen or otherwise diverted."

U.S. goods for sale in village black market.

January 10, 1967:

> ➤ *U.N. Secretary-General U Thant expressed doubts that Vietnam is essential to the security of the West.*

> ➤ *President Johnson declared during his State of the Union address "We will stand firm in Vietnam...We are in Vietnam because the United States of America and our allies are committed by the SEATO Treaty to 'act to meet the common danger' of aggression in Southeast Asia.*

> ➤ *President Johnson asked for enactment of a 6 percent surcharge on personal and corporate income taxes to help support the Vietnam War for two years, or "for as long as the unusual expenditures associated with our efforts continue."*

> *Note: Congress delayed for almost a year, but eventually passed the surcharge. The estimated expenditure in Vietnam for the 1967 fiscal year was $21 billion.*

January 11, 1967: a public observation made by a government official questioned whether the Congress or the American people had been told about the administration embarking on a major military operation in the Mekong Delta, referring to operation Song Than / Deckhouse V.

January 12, 1967 enemy forces attacked Binh Thuy airfield near Can Tho, Phong Dinh Province, with 50 rounds of mortar and recoilless rifle fire resulting in light damage to the airfield, buildings and aircraft.

January 13, 1967

Dearest Darling,

I got back from Peason Ridge this morning at 10:30 and just had time now to sit down and write after cleaning up all my equipment. Right now its 7:45 PM and I'm really tired. It really wasn't as bad as I thought it would be. I'll try to describe the chain of events as it happened this week.

Last Sunday we pulled out of the company area at 1:00 PM. We took a truck convoy to our administrative camp. Now try to picture this as a combat situation.

An administrative camp is nothing more than a briefing and training camp so the soldiers know what to expect when they get in combat. The first night at the admin camp we went on a night compass course. That's where a guy takes you out in a truck and lets you and a buddie off with nothing but a compass and an azimuth to follow. An azimuth is the number of degrees or direction to follow. It was pitch black and Steve and I started the course. It was a little over 2 miles long and it took us about an hour and a half to finish it. It was so dark that the very first step I took from the starting point I fell in a ditch. Steve saw me fall in it and started laughing and he thought he would go around it so he took one step to the right and fell in another ditch. Boy did I have the last laugh.

The only way we could keep on the right course is because of the luminous dial on the compass. If it wasn't for that we would have been lost. Out of 215 guys only 2 got lost and walked 15 miles and weren't found until the next day.

Monday we had practical work on booby traps in the jungle and in the villages and how to avoid them. We went to a quick fire range where we got to fire BB guns while walking through a swamp. That's when it started raining. It rained the rest of the day and all that night until time to get up. I was lucky and stayed dry. Also on Monday we had a class on how to raid and search a village. The villages are really authentic looking and are made with bamboo and banana leaves. The village had tunnels dug in it and we had to search them. Don't worry because we didn't get gassed all the time we were out there.

Tuesday morning we rolled up our tents and put them in our duffle bags because from then on we had to sleep in foxholes.

We loaded up on trucks again and moved to a new area that supposedly had enemy troops in that location. It didn't rain Tuesday but it was cloudy and cold.

That night all hell broke loose. We were supposed to be on 100% alert until 12:00 midnight . Then from 12:00 AM to 6:00 AM 50% alert meaning that one sleeps while the other watches for the enemy.

Well about 8:30 PM my squad leader asked me to go on a reconnaissance Patrol (to get information about enemy activity outside our perimeter). It lasted until 2:00 AM and when we got back to our camp there was all kinds of shooting and explosions. The enemy was trying to get through our lines and blow up our headquarters. I think I got about 45 or 50 minutes of sleep that night.

Wednesday it was really sunny and hot and again we packed up to move to a new location. This time on foot about 5 miles away. I did the same thing Wednesday as I did Tuesday and not much sleep. It was hot Thursday too. And in the morning I went on a demolition patrol and raid patrol combination.

For the demolition patrol me and two other guys got to blow up an ammunition dump. After we blew it up we went to a village and reconned it and raided it. When we got back it was time for lunch and then a class on hardening vehicles (preparing them against land mines) then back to camp.

We were on 100% alert (everybody awake) until 12:00 AM then 50% until 4:00 AM. That night it rained and I was lucky again and kept dry by putting a pocho over me and logs at the bottom of my foxhole so I wouldn't be laying in the water. Did you ever try to sleep on logs? I did get some sleep (about 2 hours) which was more than I had gotten the other two nights combined.

Today we finished the problem with the search of a friendly village and raid of an enemy village and then we headed for the barracks. Boy am I glad to be back.

...Well honey, I still don't know if I am going to Vietnam or not for sure. I'll just have to wait and see what my orders say. But remember, I don't want you to think I don't have a chance of going because it's very, very possible. There been more rumors around, but I'm not going to believe them until I have my orders in my hand. Whatever they are honey, just remember one thing, If I do go it's because somebody has to, even if I don't like the idea it's to protect America and people like my loving wife from communism. Honey, I know what it is and I know how it operates and it's not good at all. I like to love my wife the way I want and not by government control. I like the idea of someday owning our own home and working to support you and have the things we've dreamed of for so long.

Besides even if I do go theres possibilities that I'll never see any action.

Now I didn't say I was going, just that its very possible and all I ask is that you do your part at home for me while I'm gone, if I go, and I'll do my part and will return home as soon as possible.

Guess what? They've cut down the tours of duty over there from 12 months to 10 ½ months. That's something a little brighter anyway.

...I think this letter is quite long enough and I think its time that I finally got to bed... and I'm saying good night darling I'll see you soon.

All my love,

Jim

January 14, 1967: resettlement and care of refugees from allied Cedar Falls began with anticipation that this resettlement may become the archetype for large scale relocation of VC, from controlled villages to government areas.

January 15, 1967

Dearest Darling,

I would have written sooner but I finally got a weekend pass and decided to wait until I could tell you what we did.

Yesterday we left Ft Polk at 2:00 PM and went to Leesville, a little Army town outside the post. Well there was seven of us guys that went and we walked around for awhile then I went into my first bar. All of us sat down and I ordered a whiskey sour. After we had one drink we went to Alexandria about 6 miles away. We rented two rooms adjoining and then went to dinner in the hotel restaurant. After dinner we went to a pool hall then back to the hotel to the cocktail lounge.

I had one more drink there and then came up to my room to watch television because I'm the only married one in the group and the others wanted to go out and pick up some girls and get drunk.

I would have written last night but I didn't have a pen so I called my mom. By the way remind me to let you read a letter from my mom about you. It sure makes me feel good to know that my mom thinks of you so highly and you really didn't think so.

Back to the wild weekend, after I called mom I laid down on my bed to wait for the guys to come back and it's a good thing I didn't get drunk because the other guys came back really drunk and loud and we almost got kicked out if it wasn't for me trying to keep them quiet.

I'm attached to the 90th RG Replacement Division but it still doesn't say where I am going yet. Now they have the 90 RG Replacement Division all over the world so I'm still not sure. Now don't worry if I do go because I saw the news on television last night and it said with stepped up bombing raids the war will be over in Vietnam in 90 days or less but even with the war over I might still have to go just to make sure that all of the guerilla fighters get the word of the peace treaty. Now that's not as bad as it could be and besides the 90RG Replacement Division replaces everybody in different units like cooks, radar, intelligence, supply, and all sorts of other people that have to be replaced sooner or later. Theres less than half the people in Vietnam that are actually doing the fighting so you never can tell.

Stop- I know exactly what you are thinking "With our kind of luck you know the first place I'm going," but darling you just can't keep saying that, because it was my luck that brought me in contact with you and I don't regret that one bit. So if I have to go over seas why should I have to regret the fact that now that I am married I must protect my wife and our future children. My wife and my children will <u>never</u> see Communism or its principles.

I know I sound like I'm probably crazy with patriotism toward my country but I just want the best for my wife and children. To hell with everyone else.

Now back to brighter subjects until I find out the official word.

...(referring to a picture he sent to Micki) As you can see my ring is on and always is. That's where it will stay forever and ever. Darling if you could have seen me this weekend you would have been so proud of me. I didn't even care what the others guys thought when I told them to go out and have a good time that I was staying in the hotel room to write my wife a letter.

They might call me a wet blanket but at least I'm a <u>true</u> wet blanket and Steve will tell you that when you meet him on my next leave.

With these words of true love and meaningful affection I say good night darling, see you real soon. Sooner than you realize I'll bet.

My love to you,
Jim

January 16, 1967: a memo from the DCI (Director of Criminal Intelligence) for the President estimated that the bombing of North Vietnam had produced approximately 29,000 total casualties (killed and injured) from the beginning of Rolling Thunder in February 1965 through September 1966. Reporting approximately 11,000 were military and 18,000 were logistics workers and other civilians.

January 17 1967

My Darling Wife,

...Don't you want to be surprised when I come home? You might have to be because I don't know when I can catch a plane home. But it will be before Sunday.

I do have a surprise for you. Guess what kind of hat I have to wear home. Yep! That real stupid looking one. I had to turn in my other one. So I guess you do get some kind of surprise.

Please don't worry if I get home Sunday because before I leave the airport I will call and tell you where and when I'm coming in.

Well darling, I must close for the night and will write one more letter before I come home and I hope to enclose some more pictures if the sun comes out.

I didn't mean to sound cruel or selfish honey (referring to his weekend out) but after Peason I had to have a rest.

Please remember that you are the only one for me and I never have or ever will go out and cheat on you. Will you please get that through your head.

All my love forever,
Jim

P.S. my name was put in for promotion to P.F.C. and I just might be wearing my stripes when I come home.
Me
P.P.S. I also received my goodie package yesterday. Thank you so much, it was delicious and the thing was cute. I kept it ...
Me again

January 18 1967

Dear Sweetheart,

Just a letter begging forgiveness for last weekend. Also wishing you a Happy Anniversary. I think I beat you this time.

This will probably be a very short letter because I just got back from the laundrymat and took a shower and its about 10:30 P.M.

Friday we graduate and I'm looking forward to that day when I can once again join you. My orders still haven't come in yet and I might have to wait here for them. I hope not.

Guess what, I don't think I got that promotion. One of the clerks was talking to a bunch of us guys and said that only the squad leaders got promoted. I hope hes wrong because I sure would like to wear stripes home on leave. Maybe it would make up for that stupid hat.

Remember honey that I love you very much and I'm sorry , I won't ever go out on a weekend pass with the guys again. I didn't realize that it upset you so much.

I promise that I will call just before I come home but I might not be able to leave until Sunday so please don't worry.

Well today we turned in all our field equipment. I'm sure glad to get rid of it too.

Another thing I found out today is that all of the unmarried men are going to the 90th Replacement Division and the married ones are going to the 90th AG Replacement Division. I wonder what the difference is? It sounds like its in my favor though so I'm not going to complain.

Honey I have to close for now so please don't ever forget that I love you deeply and will be home soon to prove it.

All my love,

Jim

January 18, 1967:

> ➤ U.S. Ambassador in Bangkok, Mr. Graham A. Martin, disclosed that the United States had over 35,000 troops in Thailand.

> ➤ North Vietnamese Government documents claimed 50% of Hanoi population, mostly women and unemployed, had been evacuated due to heavy U.S. bombing in mid December 1966.

January 19, 1967: Operation Pickett, a 1st Brigade, 101st Airborne Division 42 day search and destroy mission in Kontum Province terminated.

January 20-28: 9th Infantry Division Operation Colby, a cordon and search mission in the Phuoc Chi Secret Zone made its first significant contact with the Viet Cong; 14 enemy killed.

January 26, 1967:

> ➤ report of Brigadier General Nguyen Ngoc Loan, Head of the Directorate General of National Police and Chief of the Military Security Service was involved in a wide gamut of political activities and used his position as a senior security official to apply political pressure.

> ➤ Secretary Rusk stated before a Joint Session of the legislation with regards to building a durable peace in Vietnam, "Obviously the first essential in building a durable peace is to eliminate aggression – by

preventing it, if possible, and by repelling it when it occurs or is threatened.

January 30, 1967:

➢ *500 troops guarded Saigon University's School of Medicine prepared for possible disruptive efforts by students during the public installation of a new five-man governing committee for the University.*

➢ *information reported that a large-scale Cheiu Hoi program was underway in an effort to capitalize on the upcoming New Year or Tet.*

January 31, 1967:

➢ *3rd and 4th Marines Operation Prairie 181-day search & destroy operation in Quang Tri Province terminated. Friendly losses were 255 killed, 1,159 wounded and one missing. Enemy losses were 1,397 killed, 27 POWs, 110 detained.*

➢ *In a memo from George W. Allen, Vietnamese Affairs Staff of the Office of the DCI, to Walt W. Rostow, Special Assistant to the President, reported infiltration of North Vietnamese communist forces into the Republic of Vietnam total by end of 1966 was 77,726.*

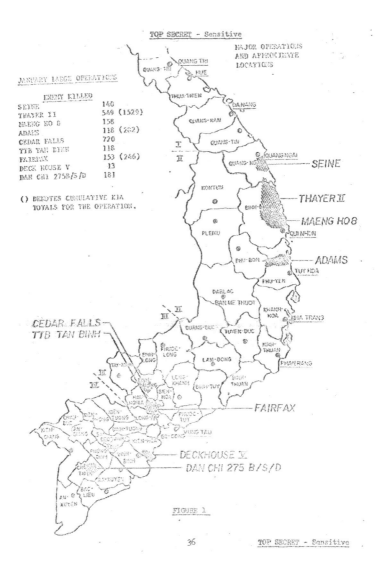

MAJOR OPERATIONS
AND APPROXIMATE
LOCATIONS

JANUARY LARGE OPERATIONS

ENEMY KILLED

SEINE	140
THAYER II	549 (1529)
MAENG HO 8	158
ADAMS	118 (202)
CEDAR FALLS	720
TTB TAN BINH	118
FAIRFAX	153 (246)
DECK HOUSE V	13
DAN CHI 275B/5/D	181

( ) DENOTES CUMULATIVE KIA
TOTALS FOR THE OPERATION.

—— SEINE

—— THAYER II

—— MAENG HO 8

—— ADAMS

CEDAR FALLS ——
TTB TAN BINH ——

—— FAIRFAX

—— DECKHOUSE V
DAN CHI 275 B/S/D

FIGURE 1

January 1967 Large Operations

In Country

"At times the fear may vanish but it doesn't stay away too long. I am always running into fear every time I turn a corner. It is just like a big blanket that falls down on your unit whenever you first hear the crackle of rifle fire."

(Excerpt from letter written April 2, 1967 to Jim's brother)

ADMINISTRATIVE DIVISIONS
SOUTH VIETNAM

Da Lat AUTONOMOUS MUNICIPALITY

0   25   50   75   100 MILES
0 25 50 75 100 KILOMETERS

QUANG TRI
Hue
THUA THIEN

I CORPS

Da Nang
QUANG NAM

QUANG TIN

QUANG NGAI

KONTUM

BINH DINH
Qui Nhon

PLEIKU

PHU BON

PHU YEN

DARLAC

KHANH HOA
Nha Trang

QUANG DUC

TUYEN DUC
Da Lat

NINH THUAN
Cam Ranh

PHUOC LONG

BINH LONG

TAY NINH

LAM DONG

BINH DUONG

LONG KHANH

BINH TUY

BINH THUAN

II CORPS

HAU NGHIA

BIEN HOA

SAIGON

CHAU DOC

KIEN PHONG

KIEN TUONG

LONG AN

GIA DINH

PHUOC TUY

AN GIANG

DINH TUONG

GO CONG

Vung Tau

III CORPS

SA DEC

VINH LONG
My Tho

CAPITAL SPECIAL ZONE

Rach Gia

KIEN GIANG

PHONG DINH
Can Tho

KIEN HOA

CHUONG THIEN

VINH BINH

BA XUYEN

BAC LIEU

IV CORPS

AN XUYEN

Chapter Six

FEBRUARY 1967

"If anybody asks me about Vietnam all I'm going to say is that I've been there."

"I've made up my mind though, that I walked into this place and I'm going to walk right back out when my time is up."

February 1, 1967:

> ➤ *CINCPAC (Commander in Chief US Pacific Command) requested authorization to conduct offensive mining against the North Vietnamese ports citing "Closure of the port of Haiphong to ocean going ships is of paramount importance and would be effective in compounding NVN logistic problems...Closure of NVN ports would be a sign of U.S. determination to prosecute the war successfully thus bringing increased pressure on Hanoi to terminate hostilities...an effective means of depriving the enemy of imports required to continue the war."*

> ➤ *Operation Prairie II, a 46 day search and destroy mission, began in Quang Tri Province.*

February 2, 1967: President Johnson publicly stated there were no "serious indications that the other side is ready to stop the war."

February 6, 1967:

> ➤ *Operation Greenleaf, a search and destroy mission in the Bin Son and Nhon Trach Districts of Bien Hoa Province began aimed at preventing Viet Cong movement during the Tet holiday.*

> ➤ *reports indicated that as many as 8,000 people may have been displaced by Operation Cedar Falls; an allied operation against a Viet Cong sanctuary north of Saigon.*

February 8, 1967: Allied forces began observance of a four-day cease fire for TET, the lunar New Year. The truce period was marked by 183 minor and 89 significant cease fire violations.

February 9, 1967: documents received by the United States Intelligence Board (USIB) stated that "During 1966 the infiltration of almost 78,000 men into South Vietnam had been reported. US military authorities, as of January 25, 1967, had confirmed the infiltration of about 39,500 of these and accepted as 'probable' the infiltration of another 10,000. The remaining 28,000 were listed in the 'possible' category."

February 13, 1967:

- ➤ *due to the failure of peace negotiations President Johnson announced that the US would resume full-scale bombing of North Vietnam.*

- ➤ *Operation Pershing began in the Bong Son Plain in northern Binh Dinh Province. 1st Cav committed all three brigades of its division. ARVN soldiers familiar with the methods of the Viet Cong operations in the Bong Son Plain helped the sky troopers locate and eliminate the numerous caves and tunnels infiltrated by the enemy. For nearly a year the division scoured the Bong Son Plain, Ahn Lo valley and the hills of coastal II Corps, seeking out enemy units and their sanctuaries. Pershing became a long and tedious mission that produced 18 major engagements and many minor skirmishes in the 11 month campaign.*

PFC James Dennis Piper's tour began February 17, 1967.

February 21, 1967

My Darling,

I hope this year will go by as fast as some of the guys tell me it does. As always I'm constantly thinking of you and wishing I were home.

I guess its best to tell you now what I'll be doing all the time I'm here. Now please don't worry or get upset because I know this will be hard to understand.

I <u>am</u> in a fighting unit as an infantry soldier just as I was trained to be. As you are reading this you are probably crying as I did when I found out that I had to tell you. But its better that I tell you now than let you find out later.

All my time here I will only spend 3 ½ months out in the field and I don't know what time or when I am going. The rest of the time I'll be safe and sound back at the main camp.

If you don't hear from me regularly its probably because I'm out in the field and don't have time to write as often as I would like to. But when I'm back here at base camp I'll really make up for the letters I haven't answered.

All I ask is that you keep writing as often as possible to keep up my moral so I don't get depressed and really start feeling sorry for myself because that's when guys don't think clearly.

I've made up my mind though, that I walked into this place and I'm going to walk right back out when my time is up.

Well now to some brighter subjects. You will probably be receiving about $150.00 every month starting around April 15 not including your allotment check of $95.20 for a grand total of $245.20 to do with as you see its needed. Plus an $18.75 savings bond every month. I'm not exactly sure of the amount but it will be in the $200.00 range. The only thing I ask is that you do save the savings bonds for our childrens' education or as a wedding present to them.

Actually, Vietnam isn't as bad as I pictured it would be. The guys in my outfit are all helping me out by giving me pointers and do's and don'ts and they seem to be working out.

I guess its about time I give you my permanent address.

PFC James D. Piper
US 56822929
Co. A 1st Bn. 8th Cav.
1st Cav. Div. Airmobile
APO San Francisco, 96490

By the way I am a PFC now and in the 1st Cavalry Division. Don't worry about the airmobile unit because it doesn't mean airborne, it means they use helicopters for supplies and stuff like that.

The 1st Cavalry insignia patch looks like this:

I guess its about time I give you my permanent address.

PFC James D. Piper
US 56022929
Co. A 1st. Bn. 8th Cav.
1st Cav. Div. Airmobile
APO San Francisco 96490

By the way I am a PFC now and in the 1st. Cavalry Division. Don't worry about that airmobile unit because it doesn't mean airborne. It means they use Helicopters for supplies and stuff like that.

The 1st Cavalry insignia patch looks like this: Its yellow y with black

markings on it. Its so big that I could sew two of them together and make a shirt of it.

Tell my parents that I'll write them as soon as I get a chance which will probably be tomorrow to let them now how things are going.

Its yellow with black markings on it. Its so big that I could sew two of them together and make a shirt of it.

Tell my parents I will write them as soon as I get a chance which will probably be tomorrow to let them know how things are going.

Right now darling I'm going to have to close.

Please don't worry too much honey because you will make yourself real sick. Just write normally as if I wasn't even here and it will make you and I feel much better.

I'll always love you darling and remember I'll never ever cheat or even think about it. You know why. I love you with all my heart and will do it automatically forever.

All my love and much more,
Jim
P.S. Say "hi" to all for me.

February 21, 1967: Student and Buddhist leaders met to organize their efforts to revive the struggle movement and to arouse protests against the Government of Vietnam. Both groups apparently expected interference by the Vietnamese security services.

■■■

February 22, 1967:

➢ *The largest U.S. military offensive of the war occurred. Operation Junction City involved 22 U.S. and four South Vietnamese battalions in an attempt to destroy the NVA's Central Office headquarters in South Vietnam. The offensive included the only parachute assault by U.S. troops during the entire war.*

➢ *Joint Chiefs of Staff (JCS) recommend 'Practice Nine Requirements Plan' not be approved. (Practice Nine was a proposed ground barrier across South Vietnam and an air support barrier across Laos. The ground barrier would consist of a series of strong points and fortified bases along the DMZ manned by combat troops.)*

➢ *Chairman Joint Chiefs of Staff forwarded his dissent to JCSM, recommended implementation of 'Practice Nine Requirements Plan.'*

February 23, 1967

Hello Mrs. Wonderful,

Here is my unit patch for you. See what I mean about big. I can't wear it here because its too bright. I have to wear a camouflaged one. I'll send one of those too later, as soon as I get an extra one.

I miss you very much. It seems like I've been here for a year already. Maybe its because I'm not as close to home as I would like to be.

Some of the guys that have just come back from the field say that our outfit hasn't been seeing too much action and probably won't which suits me just fine.

Nobody reads funny papers anymore. All they do is send home for newspaper clippings of the War in Vietnam and things Johnson says then they laugh their heads off when they read them cause ¾ of it isn't true. I do admit there is a lot of risk and danger just being here but not as much as it may seem at home. I'll just be glad when my time is up and I'm home for good. If anybody asks me about Vietnam all I'm going to say is that I've been there.

This isn't a war we're fighting. It's a big joke that happened to be played on good American men by the asshole leaders of our country.

If it was up to Kennedy or General Westmoreland I don't think I or and other G.I.'s would be here.

The only thing Johnson is worried about for dropping the big bomb is that he's afraid of killing a lot of innocent Vietnamese people. But while we're wasting our time here, a lot of American's are losing their lives for his stupid decisions. Also hes afraid of what our allies would say if we pulled out now. He thinks that they would lose confidence in the United States. Or if anything like that happened in other countrys if we would repeat the same actions there and leave the country helpless.

Vietnam isn't like other countrys or our allies because this country is so undeveloped that if we would drop an H bomb on it we wouldn't be losing anything but rather gaining a lot more respect from other countries.

Look at what happened at Hiroshima during WWII. The Japanese were more than willing to surrender after the bomb. And I think the same would happen here if they tried it.

That one bomb killed 600,000 innocent Japanese people, but it opened Japan's eyes so wide that they were able to see the dotted line on the peace treaty to sign it. And nobody else said a word about it. It would just take one bomb on Hanoi and that would almost end the war. Well enough of Vietnam from the average G.I. position.

A guy just sold me some Vietnamese money so you can have that too. Its 30 dong worth about 20¢ American money.

...You should see my jungle boots. They are comfortable and I will try to draw what they look like. They are part canvas and part leather.

Well darling I have to get ready for my training tomorrow write more later.

Hi again, I'm all packed up and ready to go but not willing. They say that the training is tougher and more dangerous than going out in the field.

If my letters seem short right now, its because stationary is very hard to get. My pen just ran out of ink and I'll have to get another one before I go to the field.

Right now I'm stationed at An Khe east of Plieku below the Demilitarized Zone. The base camp of where the operations for field exercises is at a place called English. I don't think its on the map but you can check.

I really miss you honey and wish I were home with you again. Most of the guys here now only have a short time to go.

Most, less than 30 days and I'm wishing I was in their place. But in a few short months I will be in their place and talking to the new replacements just like they are doing. I've never seen a bunch of happier guys.

Well darling its time to close again but I will write as soon as I get another chance. Probably after my training which is 3 days long.

My love forever and ever,

Jim

P.S. I love you Mrs. J.D. Piper

My love forever and ever

Jim

P.S. I love you Mrs. J.D. Piper X

February 26, 1967

Hi Sweetie,

I just got back from my training. It was just like going through A.I.T. again only not as long. It was just a review of everything I have learned so far.

I wish I could send some pictures home but I don't have any film and for a swinger its awfully hard to get. The P.X. doesn't stock enough of it and it seems like everyone that has a swinger is out of luck.

If you decide to send me any packages, please try not to send them if I can't use it up in a hurry. Don't worry about things like cigarettes or candy or canned goods because I don't have a place to put them and they will just get stolen if I leave them laying around. Also I won't be able to carry too much if I'm out in the field.

Are you counting the days until I'm home? I'm counting them and so far its gone pretty fast. Although I've only been here for 9 days. I will be home on Feb. 17, 1968 for a leave anywhere from 31 to 45 days, then I'll go to my next duty station in the states for 4 months. After that I'll be home for good. I'm getting excited about that already. Too bad it isn't closer.

I'm going to put in for my R & R for Hawaii. If I get it there will you come to see me? I sure would like to see you after about seven months of this hell hole. Its only a five minute drive from there to Waikiki and everything is cut rate for the G.I.'s on R & R so it would be fairly cheap.

Tomorrow I will be going out in the boonies* to join the rest of the company. I will be out there until June 15 and then we will come in and guard this base camp for awhile. If we are lucky we might stay at base camp for the remainder of my tour. I'm keeping my fingers crossed. I also heard some talk about the 1ˢᵗ Cavalry will be pulling out and going to some other country in a couple of months. If that happens I get to go too because I'm assigned to their outfit. Wherever they go I go.

Please don't forget to write me and tell me how much that check is for each month starting April 15. Your allotment check should still come on the 1st of each month along with the savings bond. Then on the 15th you will get another one.

I miss you so much darling. I wish I could hold you and kiss you every night. But I guess I will just have to send my love for you in letters for awhile again. XXXXXXXXX Thats only one kiss per day but I can guarantee that I will collect on every one of them when I get home. I'll send a kiss coupon every time I write a letter so you can save them and force me to pay up. Ok?

Darling its time for me to get a talk from the 1st Sergeant before I leave tomorrow so I'll have to close.

Remember that I love you very much and don't worry because nothing is going to happen to me. I'm no worse off here than driving on the freeway at home and you know I'm a safe driver.

All my love forever,
Jim

all my love forever
Jim

```
X xxxXxxxX xxxXx xxxXx
X 9x's  Kiss Coupon   9x's X
X          worth          X
X                         X
X       9 Kisses  on or   X
X 9x's about Feb 17, 1968  9t's X
Xx xxxXxxx xt Xx xxx VxxX
```

Save for the valuable special offer only given to those who have at least 300 kisses worth of these x coupons.

Love ya honey,
Me

boonies : colloquial shortening of boondocks c.1965, originally among U.S. troops in Vietnam War in ref. to the rural areas of the country, as opposed to Saigon.

February 28, 1967: in a lengthy presentation to the President from White House staffer R.W. Komer titled 'Vietnam Prognosis for 1967-68' Komer stated "getting greater efficiency out of the 700,000 men we're already supporting and financing is the cheapest and soundest way to get results in pacification."

Chapter Seven

MARCH 1967

"I live letter to letter instead of day to day."

March 1967: documents captured in South Vietnam indicated that the Viet Cong were experiencing difficulty keeping certain units up to strength and manpower, causing deterioration in the quality of local and irregular forces. Though a statement made by a white house official stated, "There is as yet no indication that manpower will force the Viet Cong to curtail their combat operations."

March 1, 1967

Hi Honey,

Well I'm in the field with my unit. I haven't received any mail from you yet. I'm going to rewrite my address for you and add 2nd Platoon so it will get to me faster.

P.F.C. James D. Piper
US 56822929 2nd Platoon
Co. A 1st Bn 8th Cav
1st Cav Division Airmobile
APO San Francisco 96490

Honey this place is really beautiful. The only bad thing about it is the war and the poverty stricken people.

They say that our company sees very little action because all they do is go through villages and pick up suspects. We've already been through about 10 villages in 2 days and my feet are killing me.

I had my first helicopter ride yesterday but it wasn't a joy ride. It was a combat air assault. They call all their airlifts combat air assaults but all it is, is hitchhiking from one place to another.

After a couple of months we will be going to base camp at An Khe to guard the green line around the border. Its real easy because theres nothing to do. The guys that are there now just write letters and listen to radios. I'm looking forward to that.

I don't know what to tell you about how it is here because every day it changes. Sometimes it seems real quiet and peaceful. Then other times all hell breaks loose. I can hear the artillery going off in the distance all night long.

Please don't worry about me. I'll be alright I have 3 lucky charms and a good reason to come back home safe and sound.

My lucky charms are your class ring, your mom's silver dollar and an old horse shoe I found at An Khe.

My one good reason is you my darling. We have so many plans that have to be done and carried out to make our lives happy forever.

I still haven't received any mail from you today but maybe it will come in with our dinner meal on a helicopter. We get a hot meal once a day flown in by helicopter and our mail comes in twice a day.

Sweetie I have to close now. Keep praying for me. <u>I love you Mrs. Piper.</u>

My love forever,

Jim

March 2, 1967

My darling wife,

Just some words of love to let you know I'm alright and I still love you and always will. Yesterday I took my first shower since I left home.

It really wasn't a shower but a bath. I went into the river to wash up and it sure felt good.

I had to change pens because the other one wasn't working.

I wasn't going to tell you but you might as well know that I'm not over here to play games. My first night out in the field we were pinned down by a squad of North Vietnamese Regulars. That was the worst fire fight the 1st Cavalry had seen since they got here and I made it through without a scratch. My sergeant told me that if I made it through that battle , I'd have no trouble getting home safely as long as I keep following orders. From now on we will probably not run into a situation like that again because our company is on a new mission, to search and clear villages and take as many prisoners as possible.

Now that I told you that you are probably scared to death that I might get hurt. But as I said before, that was the worst and the only one they have had in 6 months. They keep telling me I'm a damn good soldier and I will never see another fight like that as long as I'm here.

The reason I didn't tell you right away was because I thought you would think I was lying if I told you nothing was happening. That would just make you worry more. And its better that you hear whats going on from me than someone else who doesn't know for sure.

I'm sorry these are short letters sweetheart but I haven't got enough time to write longer ones like I want to. After I get to the Green Line I'll have all the time I need. That's when you will receive some of the best letters I will ever write.

As long as I'm still writing and letting you know that I'm safe and sound there is nothing to worry about. Just remember that if you don't get a letter as often as you would like to, I'm still thinking of you and loving you. I look at your picture everyday and am looking forward to when I can see you in person once again, forever.

All my everlasting love,
Jim

March 2, 1967: Two USMC companies on operation Prairie II engaged an NVA company in the vicinity of Hill 124 resulting in 109 enemy killed.

March 3, 1967: aerial observation spotted an estimated 250 enemy on a trail northwest of Quang Tri City and 50-60 more one kilometer west. Artillery and air strikes were called on both groups. Results were 70 enemy killed and no friendly casualties.

March 4, 1967

Dearest Darling,

I've got some good news for you. Today we got on some helicopters and came back to An Khe to run patrol on the perimeter. I sure am glad to get out of the boonies. We will still be sleeping out in the open but at least it's a lot safer around An Khe. That should make you feel better.

Last night I had to check out a small cave. I was real scared so I took at shotgun and a flashlight with me as I poked my head in the cave. I didn't see anything but I told the sergeant I heard something moving in there and didn't want to go in. So I took a hand grenade and pulled the pin. My sergeant told me I only had four seconds to get out of the cave after I throw the grenade. I had quite a ways to go after I threw it to get clear of the blast, almost 20 yards. This is what it looked like.

Last night I had to check out a small cave. I was real scared so I took a shotgun and a flashlight with me as I poked my head in the cave. I didn't see anything but I told the sargeant I heard something moving in there and didn't want to go in. So I took a hand grenade and pulled the pin. My sargeant told me that I only had four seconds to get out of the cave after I through the grenade. I had quite a ways to go after I threw it to get clear of the blast, almost 20 yards. This is what it looked like.

cave   gulley   20 yards away

I crawled into the cave and threw the grenade, then I ran and jumped into the

I crawled into the cave and threw the grenade, then I ran and jumped into the gulley and still had 3 seconds to go after I was safe from the blast. That's how fast I moved.

As it turned out there wasn't anything in the cave anyway. But I was still scared.

Right now I'm back at base camp in An Khe in a barracks with an air mattress as snug as a bug in a rug. All I've been thinking about is you and home. I wish I could be there with you right now.

It sure is lonely here in hell.

I haven't received any mail from you yet but it should be coming in pretty soon. The guys have been telling me it takes 3 to 4 weeks to regulate the mail system after a new man enters the company so I guess I'll be hearing from you real soon.

Yesterday we caught two prisoners. A young man about 25 or 30 and an old one about 55.

We didn't want to take the old one with us because he was too old to be a Viet Cong. But when we took the young one he started crying and hollering. I guess he didn't want to be separated. The old man was like he was in his second childhood. He wet and messed his pants and our squad had to guard him. Boy did he stink.

I got a souvenir to bring home with me. Its an old kerosene lamp with a wick. It still works but the handle is broken. I guess the base is made of real china. It doesn't have any writing on it to say where it came from. I'm going to send it home when I get to the post office soon. If I do, please don't let Mikie touch it because its real old. I found it in a Vietnamese village in the Bon Son Valley.

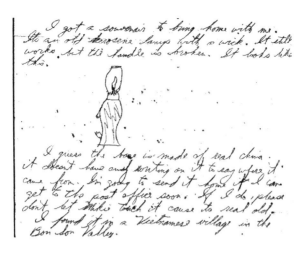

I got a souvenir to bring home with me. Its an old kerosene lamp with a wick. It still works but the handle is broken. It looks like this.

I guess the base is made of real china. It doesn't have any writing on it to say where it came from. I'm going to send it home if I can get to the post office soon. If I do, please don't let Mike touch it cause its real old. I found it in a Vietnamese village in the Bon Son Valley.

If I can find any more souvenirs I'll try to send them home as soon as possible. Some of them could be worth a lot of money. The lamp can't be worth as much because its not in perfect condition and there are lots more where it came from. But I still would like to save it for a memento.

The next time I go into a village I'll try to find an evil spirits banner to send you. Its supposed to chase away evil spirits and bring good luck to the family. Some of them are beautiful. But most are just plain looking. The Vietnamese aren't very artistic. One thing I've got to say for these people and that is that they are good farmers.

The day before yesterday I was in a village and the children came up to me and asked me for cigarettes and candy. I didn't have any and felt sorry for them so I gave them some instant coffee. I don't know what they did with it but I know it doesn't taste good.

Then an old woman about 65 wanted some gum. I gave it to her but she didn't have any teeth to chew it with. I wish I could understand their language because the gum was stale and hard and it sounded like she was cussing me out. I just laughed at her. She was kind of pathetic looking as I walked off laughing while she was trying to chew that gum.

Every village we have been in there hasn't been any men. Unless we catch them by surprise. All there has been is old women and real young children. Sometimes we will find an old man that is too old to fight so hes left in the village with the women and the children.

Well sweetie its time for me to end this chapter of my war stories for now. Please write soon. I love you more than the distance I am from you and that's quite a lot.

All my everlasting love,

Jim

P.S. Write soon honey.

Love, Me

Micki has saved that lamp all these years. This photo was taken 7-31-11.

March 5, 1967

Hi Sweets,

Well I was only in An Khe for one day but at least we didn't go back to the boonies. Right now we are pulling guard on the Green Line Out Post.

Its pretty good duty because I'll get to write more often now. At least for a few days anyway. You never can tell what we'll be doing next.

...I hope the weeks go by as fast as these last 2 have gone. Do you know that I only have 49 weeks 6 days and 5 hours before I leave here.

If you think about it, it doesn't seem as long as it is. I've got a real good chance of becoming a sergeant before I leave here because in June most of the guys will be leaving and the company is going to need some leadership for the replacements. I know one more thing for sure and that is that I will be a spc 4 when I get home. It's the same rank as Corporal.

Guess what I just figured out how many weeks I've got before I get out of the Army for good. Only 75 weeks to go. When I get back to the states I'll probably have to go to Ft Polk or Ft Lewis. I asked for Ft Ord but I don't think I'll get it because the form I filled out said to pick a place that corresponds with my job in the Army. I think Ft Ord is just for basic training and not A.I.T. for infantry. I won't mind as long as I'm in the states again.

Well honey its getting dark so I'll continue the letter tomorrow morning.

Love ya lots,
Me

Hi again honey,

Does the time seem to be dragging to you? Its not for me. Maybe its because I'm being kept busy.

Honey I think that I finally realize what it takes to be a man in the world.

Almost every generation of people have had contact with or felt the deep cuts of war. I'm no exception to the rule. Believe me this is no place for immature kids.

My prime concern is to be able to come back to you alive so I can once again hold you in my arms. But this time you will find a big change because I will be a man then.

All my life I've been waiting to grow up and assume responsibilities of a wife and children and a home.

Within the 2 weeks I have been here, my whole outlook on life has changed. I'm not the boy that left you but the man who is coming back safe and sound.

All the plans we've made together are going to be carried out to the best of my ability for your security and welfare. All I ask in return is the love, attention and moral support to help me do these things for us and our children. Theres no doubt in my mind that we will be on top of the world in a few short years of hard work.

Do you think you know what I said or didn't it make sense? Sometimes I just write what I think and forget about grammar or types of words I use.

My love darling, I give to you willingly, faithfully and unendingly through my year of hardship over here especially and forever and ever. I think of you and dream of you constantly through my limited days in hell on earth.

Please expect me for dinner on Feb 18, 1968 because I will be there alive and well.

Loving your enormously,

Jim

March 6, 1967: CIA Document stated that "the overall US effort is having a much greater impact on the overall capabilities of the Viet Cong, including the guerilla effort, than is commonly realized.'

March7- April 18 1967: a 40-day search and destroy operation named Oh Jak Kyo I in Phu Yen Province was launched, linking the Korean Capital and 9th divisions' TAORs. Friendly losses were 23 killed and 115 wounded. Enemy losses were 831 killed, 418 detained, 630 individual and 29 crew-served weapons.

March 8 –April 8, 1967: Operation Waialua commenced, designed to stop the flow of VC supplies on the Song Vam Co Dong in Hau Nghia Province.

March 8, 1967: Congress authorized 4.5 billion for the war.

March 9, 1967

My darling wife,

Yesterday we were taken off the Long Range Out Post and put on Quick Reaction Force at base camp. Also yesterday I went on a mission. It was a fire reconnaissance mission and all of us had more fun than work.

We started walking along the highway about 8 PM and every time we would stop we would fire our weapons on automatic into the bushes then keep moving.

We walked from 8 PM 'till 12:30 AM and stopped for the night then came back from there back to base camp today.

Guess what? After 25 air assaults I'll get an air medal to wear on my uniform. I already have 5 assaults done and tomorrow it should be up to about 8.

It doesn't scare me as much as it used to because I used to hear stories about guys getting wounded while getting off helicopters but now the 1st Cavalry has gotten "chicken" and won't land anywhere that is not secure from the enemy. That's because they have lost so many helicopters and they cost the gov't $4,000,000.00 a piece.

I don't mind this kind of duty because we get to sleep in a barracks almost every night.

When I get a pass to go to An Khe I'm going to have a colored picture made of me. I'm going to send it and the lamp I've got home to you.

Well honey, it looks like I'm going to have to finish this letter tomorrow because its getting too dark to see and theres no light in this barracks...

Hooray! I finally received two letters from you and one from mom. Boy am I glad to hear from you.

Well about my R&R. I can't put in for it until the middle of May because there are many guys with more time over here than me. But if I talk to my sergeant real nice and tell him a little white lie that you are going to Hawaii with your Aunt Marion in Aug or Sept maybe he'll let me go then.

Most of the guys are getting their R&R after being here for 7 or 8 months. They say its better to wait that long so you don't have that much time left before you go home.

...Honey your whole plan about becoming parents on my R&R sounds great but I can't remember any of the names either...

Today our platoon was called out on a mission all except 8 of our best men and guess what? Your ever loving is one of those chosen few to stay back on an 8 man recon team. The same thing we did the night before last.

I like those kinds of missions because we don't have to worry about any dangerous areas to walk into.

The other day after our recon we were waiting for a ride back to camp and a beer truck came along and crossed the bridge where we had stopped. The guys that were guarding the bridge jumped on the back of the truck and threw off about 7 cases of beer. So we had a beer party while we waited for a ride.

Everything over here is fine. Things seem to be looking up all the time.

No I haven't shot any VC yet that I know of but I did shoot at them. I don't think I hit any because I kept my eyes closed and my head and ass down so it wouldn't get shot off. That was only one time and it was the first day in the company. I told you about that. We were pinned down all night long but we had the VC completely surrounded and got most of them.

We only had 4 casualties and they were just small cuts and scratches. Old Charlie doesn't know how to aim very well. Thank God. Still only 4 casualties out of 256 men is pretty good when you consider we got 42 of them and about 6 prisoners. Maybe 3 or 4 escaped. Those 3 or 4 that escaped are probably still running full speed to get away from us and we aren't even in the area anymore. That's how scared they are of the 1st Cav.

...One thing you should know right now and that is that I'm not even thinking about being a hero, especially when I've got a wife and future plans to fulfill.

Flash- called on patrol
>   All my love,
>   Jim
>   P.S I'll write tomorrow.
>   Love ya

March 9, 1967:

> ➢   *President Johnson acknowledged that US jets based in Thailand were bombing North Vietnam.*

> ➢   *Due to North Vietnam's dependence on Chinese rice supplies French officials in Hanoi believed that North Vietnam will not negotiate with the U.S. without China's approval.*

March 10, 1967: United States Vietnamese Ambassador Bui Diem met with Prime Minister Ky and reported on the 'Peace Movement' in America stating that the Vietnam War was unpopular and that if the Government of Vietnam (GVN) could not continue a trend toward stability the United States might decide to abandon the war. An advisor present took issue with Diem's statements stating that without stability "no President could help." Prime Minister Ky concurred.

March 11, 1967   344 days short

Dearest Darling,

I have received 2 more of your wonderful letters and am a very happy soldier at the moment. Its always good to hear from someone who loves you and you love them or <u>her</u>. You are so right the days just don't fly by as fast as I want them to.

It takes about one full week from the date postmarked on your letters to reach me. I imagine the packages will take a little longer.

...Believe it or not we do have tv here although I haven't seen it yet. I do listen to the radio quite often. They have their own broadcasting station for the 1st Cav in An Khe that's run by Army Disc Joskeys. Its even better than the stations at home because they play all the oldies but goodies and very popular songs back home.

You mean to tell me you really haven't cut your hair yet? Well I don't think it will be too long before you do. I know how mad you get when its too long to do anything with.

Speaking of hair, you see how long mine is getting. I might just let it grow a whole year without getting it cut. Maybe just a trim now and then but that's all.

...Guess what my sergeant did? Last night I was out on patrol and while I was gone my sergeant picked up a little orphan boy. He's about 8 or 9 years old and speaks real good English. We're going to take him to Bong Son with us when we go so he can go to school. You should see him dance. Hes just like the 'Action Kids' or 'Where the Action Is.' Do you know that Chinese fella with the Action Kids, well he dances and looks just like him. His name is "Hey Joe." He was named that after the song "Hey Joe" that hes always singing.

...Well honey the only VC I have actually seen are the prisoners and a couple of the ones that were permanently put out of action by us. I haven't seen any since I left the field over a week ago.

What I said about our outfit going to another country as far as I know is just a rumor. But I sure would like to get out of here soon.

What I meant about Waikiki is that the R & R station in Hawaii is only 5 minutes from Waikiki so we can probably see Waikiki while we're there.

From what I understand from the guys that have come back from R & R they get 7 days there. Great huh?

Well darling I'm going to have to close again so I can write and answer to your mom before I get called out on another patrol or something.

Remember that I send all my love and kisses in every letter I write to you darling. And my love continues to grow even while we are far apart.

All my love and a big kiss,
Jim

March 11, 1967: 2/5 Cav battled for Hill 82 in the Bong Son Province near the village of Phu Ninh.

March 14 1967

My darling wife,

I just received your package and was most happy and thankful because I was down to my last cigarette. I really am enjoying those cookies. The guys wanted me to tell you that they were very good. Thank you for the Vienna sausage too. I know I'm going to like that because I am getting tired of C rations.

I was very happy to receive your package, but why didn't you put a letter in it?

Honey I've got a very good chance to get Hawaii for my R & R but I can't put in for it until late in April. But don't worry I'll give you all the information you need in order to make reservations for the trip.

Darling I'm so looking forward to starting a family on my R&R. I didn't think I would be this enthuised about starting one so soon but I really am looking forward to going home after I get out of here and walk down the street arm & arm with my pregnant wife. Then I will be able to get an emergency leave when you have it.

You just don't know how proud I would be to have everybody look at you and say, "I'll bet she's going to have the cutest twin girls."

Boy! You will have to be sewing buttons on my shirts 3 times a day because I'm going to be bursting that many with pride.

Do you really think I'll make a good father? That's the only thing that really bothers me. I keep wondering if I can be stern yet gentle at the same time but always keeping the upper hand. I take that back because after what I've seen with your brother I know our kids will be well behaved.

Well now to tell you whats up around here. Tomorrow we are going back to the field. I wish we didn't have to but at least the time goes much faster for me . After we come back in this next time we should be staying in for at least 3 months guarding the An Khe bridge before we have to go out again. Then when we go out again it will be for 2 months and the next time we come in I won't have to go out anymore before I come home, because then we will be guarding the Green Line and during that time my tour will be through so I now have a total of 5 months altogether to do in the field. That's not too bad.

After my R&R I will be able to use the term the other guys are using now when their time is almost up and that is "I'm short." Meaning I get to go home soon.

...Well honey I've got to close for now so I can get that letter off to my parents...I do love you very much darling...

All my lasting love,

Jim

※※※

March 14, 1967: USN and USCG intercepted a 100-foot enemy steel-hulled trawler beached northeast of Quang Ngai city, cargo captured: 1,150 chicom carbines, 25 heavy machineguns, 29 light machineguns, 1 57mm recoilless rifle, 18 bolt-action rifles, 7,000 round of 7.62 ammunitions and 12 claymores.

▄▄▄

March 15, 1967: Da Nang Air Base was attacked with over 10 rounds of 140mm Russian spin-stabilized rockets. Sixteen US were wounded, there was negligible aircraft and runway damage. Reaction forces located 23 launchers and 11 rockets on the east bank of the Yen river, 11km southwest of the base.

※※※

March 15 – April 3, 1967: mobile guerilla Operation Blackjack 32 began, conducted by A-304 with 126 Cambodian CIDG in eastern Phuoc Tuy Province to interdict VC pathways. Use of airstrikes on April 3 smothered the advancing VC the remaining allied forces were lifted out.

March 16, 1967

Hi Sweetie,

Well I guess this will be my last letter until I get some more writing paper. I'm sorry that I didn't get a chance to write yesterday.

Well I'm now back to writing this letter. When I started we had to move out in 5 minutes so I didn't get a chance until this morning to finish.

I received your 20 page letter yesterday and believe me honey I sure enjoyed every page. I also got another letter from you and one from Ann. Please tell her that I won't be able to answer her letter because I don't have any more paper.

...Honey do you think that we could be able to start a family? You can tell better than me because you are handling the bills and have a better picture of the situation than I do. Darling I <u>want</u> to start one on my R&R. It would mean so much to us. Although I can't promise that it will be successful on my R&R I hope it is.

I'm so glad that the furniture is ours now. That's one more bill out of our way. It should make it a lot easier now for you now to bank the extra money without cutting yourself short.

Do you know those cigarettes you sent me? Well I fell in a hole filled with water and 2 packs got soaked. If you send some more, please send a few small baggies to keep them and my wallet dry in case I fall in another one.

I had been reading a book called the Ugly American and I was almost through with it and that got soaked too so I had to throw it away.

If you could see me now you would disown me. I'm filthy dirty. My hands are rough and scratched. I haven't shaved for 4 days and I stink so bad I can hardly live with myself.

I love you darling very much and I need you now more than anything else in the world.

Well I have to finish this at another time because we're pulling out in about fifteen minutes.

Hi again. We only moved a couple hundred yards so here I am trying to finish up. Please excuse the dirty paper but I can't seem to keep anything clean over here.

Honey I hate it over here and I'm scared all the time. When we go through villages and pick up suspects its not too dangerous but when we set up at night, that's when it gets scary. Every night we call in Artillery support just in case we run into "Charlie." All night long you can hear our artillery going off all around us and it sure is good to know that its on our side even if we can't get any sleep...

Honey I really can't use my swinger out here in the field because I have no place to put it. So please don't send any film for it until I ask for some OK? I've got enough soap to last me for awhile, but I do need cigarettes every so often. If you could just send 4 or 5 packs like you did before I would be very happy.

...I don't know the exact date that we will be back at base camp but I imagine it will be around June 15.

Honey I've got to move out again so I'll have to close. Please don't worry if you don't get a long letter soon. I will try to find some thing of paper to let you know I love you and am all right.

All my love forever,
Jim

P.S. I LOVE YOU,
Me

March 17, 1967: intelligence reports stated that Vietnamese Ambassador to the United States, Bui Diem questioned whether Ky will be nominated as the military's candidate; though in the event of winning the Presidency, Ky will choose Phan Quang Dan as PM although he is unpopular with intellectuals.

March 19, 1967: the Battle of Ap Bau Bang II occurred with initial VC mortar and ground attack. US and allied forces utilized 29 airstrikes and 2,148 arty rounds leaving 227 enemy dead.

March 20 – April 1, 1967: search and destroy mission Operation Beacon Hill II began in Quang Tri Province with a combined amphibious and heliborne assault by the 7th Fleet's Special Landing Force with BLT 1/4 Marines near Gio Ling just south of the DMZ.

March 21, 1967: private correspondence between President Johnson and Ho Chi Minh "...North Vietnam's position is hardening. Communist forces have become more aggressive in recent weeks; there are indications that, after a lull, infiltration may be picking up. Hanoi may also be reinforcing the DMZ. Some new weapons have been introduced in South Vietnam. In short, recent North Vietnamese actions seem to assume a further period of hightened military efforts, and probably also further American escalation."

March 22, 1967

Dearest Darling,

Please forgive me for not writing sooner but we have been in the field on the go most of the time and just recently we had another run-in with "Charlie." Don't worry if you read in the papers that the 1st cav suffered many casualties because I am perfectly alright. The worst injury I've had here so far has been mosquito bites. That's all I intend to get.

Now I am using a different weapon. Do you remember when I was in training and I shot a tree top off with a grenade launcher? Well that's the weapon I have now and I'm pretty good at it.

I've been receiving mail fairly regularly lately. I sure am glad to get it.

Are you getting real graceful for me with your hula lessons?

Honey, I did not kill any VC that I know about although I did shoot at them but couldn't see them. When we counted the dead ones after the fight it didn't seem to bother me because I just considered them as dead animals and not people. Its hard to explain but then again it's a hard war to explain.

Yesterday I received 3 letters. 1 from you, 1 from Grandma Pacheco and 1 from a woman in the trailer court where my Grandpa lives. That last one really shocked me because I have only seen her about two or three times in my life.

I should write Grandma a few lines if I get a chance today. Right now we're just about ready to move to a new village.

Darling I love you so very much that I count the hours until I can hold you again. I don't seem so far away when I get a letter from you and I live from letter to letter knowing that someday we won't ever have to write to each other anymore for the rest of our lives.

I can't wait for that day.

Honey, do I sound like I have changed at all since I have been here? The guys say that everyone changes somehow.

...Honey, this is going to have to be a short letter because we are getting ready to move.

I love you with all my heart. Please don't worry because I'm safe.

All my love,
Jim

P.S. Happy Easter next Sunday.
Love, Me.

March 22 – 25, 1967: 2/5 Marines launched search and destroy operation 'Newcastle' in the An Hoa Basin of Quang Nam Province. Friendly losses 5 KIA and 55 wounded, enemy losses were 118 KIA, 35 detained.

March 23, 1967

Dearest Darling,

I know this paper is pretty dirty but its all I could scrounge up and I just had to write to you to let you know how much I really love you and tell you that I'm allright.

You have probably read in the papers that the first cav has been hit hard and suffered many casualties. Well, its true but I'm O.K. Right now we are holding a village because this area has been declared a war zone.

The village we are in is in the Ahn Lo Valley near Bong Son.

We were preparing to go to the ocean and check out all the villages between there and the mountains when we got a call from the 2nd Battalion that they ran into VC and needed help real bad so our company commander called for some helicopters and off we went to help out.

When we got here it was pretty quiet and all we heard was a few shots from a sniper. We waited until morning then assaulted the village. That's when all hell broke loose. There was a Battalion size force of P.A.V.N's (Peoples Army of Viet Nam) that's the North Vietnamese regulars, that were camped there.

It was one of the biggest or the biggest battle that the 8th cav has ever seen. In case you are wondering, I'm not bragging because I'm still sick over it. I killed 2 gooks and wounded another. Gooks is a slang word they use for VC.

The battle itself lasted about 55 hours off and on then we have been receiving sniper fire for another 25 or 26 hours. But now everything is fairly peaceful and we will be returing to the rear area soon, however I don't know exactly when or if they are going to change their minds again and stay out here. I hope not.

Well honey this month is just about over and that leaves only 10 ½ months to go and only 5 ½ before I can see you in Hawaii.

I'm so thrilled with the idea of starting a family on my R&R and I know it wouldn't be too hard on us.

And about that job at United. I don't think it would be wise to look into until after I get my college over with to find out how the G.I will work out. If it doesn't work out the way we have planned then I can use my college education in Business Management + Supervision in almost any field I want to go into. For instance General Motors, or Real Estate, or anything. So I'm not going to look for another job unless our plans don't work out.

Hey I got a bigger pack yesterday so you can send that small recorder if you want to but you will have to send me tape and stamps so I can send it back O.K. When you send me tapes, please send enough stamps so I can send the tape you made and the one I made back because if I keep getting your tapes, I'll have no room left in my pack. So I'll send yours back along with mine. That way we can save all of them.

And about that camera. Honey you would really appreciate slide pictures from over here. Also I can tell you what they are about on the tape recorder as you look at them. Then it would be like as if I was there explaining the pictures to you. I would even number the pictures so you couldn't get lost. Darling it would be great to show our children when they are old enough to understand. Even when they start social studies in school and have to draw or build a model of a Vietnamese home as a project they could use the pictures for reference.

So help me Christ, if there is one fly in our house after we get it, I'll burn the whole house down. There are so many flies over here I could scream everytime one lands on me.

Well my darling I can't think of too much else to say.

Oh yeah. I fell into the river the other day when I was trying to cross it on a skinny log. Well the log broke and I got drenched. My wallet is a mess and all my pictures are ruined. Could you please send me another small wallet sized picture of yourself. I sure miss looking at your picture every day. About the only thing that didn't get ruined was your moms silver dollar.

Please tell everyone for me that I'm allright and not to worry too much. I'll see you soon in Hawaii.

All my love to you only,
Jim

P.S. Hey! I'm almost 20 years old. Do you know I feel like 40?
 Love you lots more,
 Me

March 23, 1967: Government reports stated that "defoliation operations in Binh Dinh Province resulted in total crop destruction in the areas affected, but in spite of this the Viet Cong (VC) in the VC-controlled areas continued military activities. After defoliation the majority of civilians moved to government of Vietnam (GVN)-controlled areas, and those who remained behind had to replant their crops with little or no help from the VC. The civilians obtained new seed from nearby villages, and the VC obtained food supplies from villages not affected by defoliation. In general, defoliation operations did not critically impede VC activities."

Note: Herbicides were used by the U.S. during the Vietnam War to defoliate the hiding places of the Viet Cong (VC) guerillas and North Vietnamese Army (NVA) regulars.

The most infamous herbicide used was called Agent Orange. The steel drums in which the herbicides were transported were color-coded with an orange stripe. Other colors such as Blue, White, Purple and Pink, were used to designate different herbicide formulations.

The largest volume of herbicide was applied from the air by C-123 "Provider" twin-engine aircraft. This air spray program was code named Operation Ranch Hand.

Herbicides were also used around the perimeters of fire bases to keep the concertina wire clear of vegetation, providing an open view for sentries on guard duty. Herbicides were also

*sprayed along river banks to reduce the number of US
casualties in the Brown Water Navy (small USN river patrol or
gun boats).*

*Below is a map of the provinces of the Central Highlands
showing the total volume sprayed of the three major herbicides
used in the war; Agents' Orange, Blue and White.*

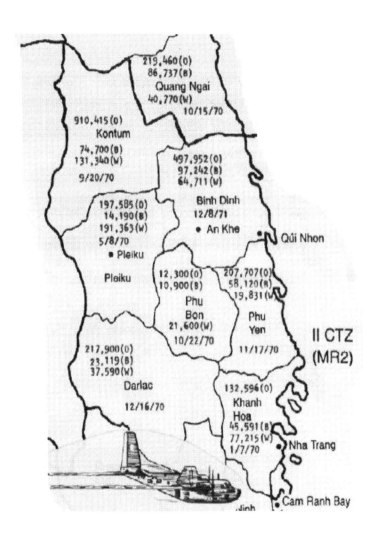

The following map is a representation of the total herbicide spray missions in Vietnam. The dark areas represent the concentrated spraying areas from fixed-wing aircraft. The map does not include spraying of perimeters by helicopters or other spraying methods.

The III Corps area received the heaviest concentrations of spraying, followed by I Corps, II Corps and IV Corps.

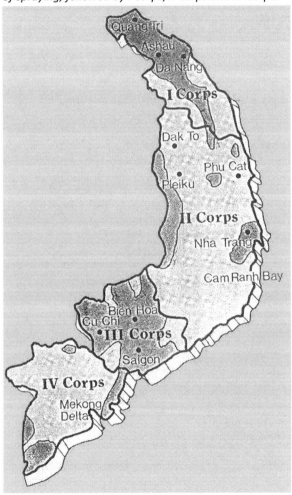

March 23, 1967: according to US intelligence, Prime Minister Ky was willing to negotiate with North Vietnam (NVN) and the National Front for the Liberation of South Vietnam (NFLSV), but he was unwilling to compromise on certain points merely to get negotiations started.

They were:

1) No coalition government with the NFLSV;

2) Full representation of GVN at negotiations;

3) NFLSV members accepted into GVN only as individuals;

4) Negotiations can start only after national elections.

March 25, 1967

My Darling Wife,

Today is Saturday and its been another routine day in the field.

I received a letter from you today and I'm glad you liked the comfort set. Next time I go to town I'll pick up a couple more sets until you have a different color for every day of the week. How would you like that?

I might get a pass on my birthday so I will be able to get them then. You said you would like it a size larger, but what if you lose some weight like you said? Then they might be too big. Maybe I can find a maternity one for when you go to the hospital for our first born.

Sorry I didn't finish this letter yesterday, but as usual we moved again and it was dark when we made camp.

Last night was real exciting (ha,ha). I was on guard and around 10:30 PM I heard a lot of commotion and people yelling "halt, "halt" then I saw what they were trying to halt. It was a North Vietnamese soldier naked from the waist down, without a weapon and running right past me. Somebody caught him, but he was only a decoy so another one could get by.

We had moved into a village where the VC were already dug in. About 20 minutes later I and 3 other guys were looking for the hole he came out of and we found some planks buried just beneath the sand. After I scraped off a few inches another guy went to pull one off and there was an explosion. We all fell back away from it. Me and the guy that pulled the board got sand in our eyes. But I'm alright. There was 2 N.V.A.'s (North Vietnamese Army) guys in the hole and one was still alive so we threw a hand grenade in it.

After clearing the bodies out we found that they were officers and the explosion was a grenade that they used to commit suicide so we wouldn't be able to beat any information out of them.

We found important documents, weapons, U.S. hand grenades, money, food and some pictures (snap shots) of Ho Chi Minh the Vietnamese Premiere at a banquet.

One of the officers was personally decorated by him.

Have you heard anything about the two major battles in the Ahn Lo Valley? Or the Battle of Binh Dinh Province? That's where I am now, but things are cooling off rapidly. Charlie Cong is on the run back to North Vietnam.

Today I got five letters. Three of them were from you darling but one of them was an old one from 90th Rep on Feb 24. The other 2 were March 21 and I think March 19 when Gary & Marsha wrote in the letter. Please thank them for me. And tell them I think of our good times with them often.

...I forgot to tell you about the other two letters. One was a nice letter from Jan and one from my Aunt Dolly. If you get a chance could you please tell them that I'll write as soon as I get an extra few minutes (but you come first.)

My Grandma from L.A. sent a real nice Easter card and I have to answer her too sometime. But I don't have enough paper or envelopes for all of them right at the moment.

I don't really know if I have to return to the field after my R&R. But I do know the later I take my R&R the better the chance of staying in the rear area.

All of the action in South Vietnam for the first cav is right here in Ahn Lo Valley, Binh Dinh Province. It's the most populated and the largest area in Vietnam.

...I can't look at furniture in Vietnam unless I go to Saigon or some big city like that. All of these other little towns are crook joints and everything is cheaply made.

Speaking of periods. Please figure out a good time for my R&R. When the time is right then we can be sure of success. Check with the doctor if you have to. I want so much to be sure it works the first time.

Well sweetie its getting dark again and I can't see too well to write so until next time.

I love you and miss you very much. Thank you for the paper I needed it badly. Now I need a couple good pens. I keep borrowing one everytime I want to write.

All my devouring love,
Jim

P.S. See you soon, Mommy to be.

Love,

        Me, again

Note:

The Battle of Binh Dinh, known as operation Byrd, consisted of one airmobile battalion task force that was detached under I Field Force control in Binh Thuan Province to support pacification activities around the city of Phan Thiet. The operation scheduled for 60 days lasted 17 months included 2d Battalion, 7th Cavalry scout section from the air cavalry squadron, a platoon of engineers, a battery of 105-mm howitzers, a platoon of aerial rocket artillery, lift helicopters, a signal team, and intelligence and civil affairs personnel, plus a forward support element for logistics. 1st Cav was given the mission of protecting the port of Phan Thiet by defeating the enemy forces in the Byrd area and opening Northern Highway #1.

Note: The Ahn Lo valley has been referred to as the 'valley of death' because it had been 'bombed and fought over until no living thing survived.'

March 25, 1967

Hi Honey,

I know you must think that I'm not writing very much but I am every chance I get. I write more letters than anyone else in my platoon. I also receive more letters. That's because I've got such a loving thoughtful wife.

I sure hope we get to go back to An Khe soon. I'm getting pretty tired of the same scenery all the time. I wish I could stay clean for at least 3 hours. I'll be looking forward to hot showers also when we get to Hawaii, but not as much as being with you on our second honeymoon. Darling its going to be wonderful, just you and I in Hawaii <u>without</u> any phone calls or doorbells to disturb us. I just hope room service doesn't pester us. That would really be funny wouldn't it?

The sergeant said that I have a very good chance of getting my R&R in late Sept or early Oct. In a way I hope its early October because then I will have that much less time to go over here when I return from R&R but I want to see you sooner than that.

I only have 329 days left and it seems to be going pretty fast. I live from letter to letter instead of day to day. I have about 189 days before I can see you again. That should be gone in no time at all. After my R&R I should have about 133 days left. That's about 4 months and 10 days.

I hope you will be 4 months and 10 days pregnant by then. It sure would be a nice coming home present. There is a possibility that I could come home after 10 months + 5 days over here if my orders come in for stateside duty. Then I'll be eligible to rotate back. It doesn't happen too often so don't get your hopes up. Still it's a nice thought.

I still like Shawna Marie as a girls name but for twins I still like Loni + Lory Lynn. Boys names are a little bit tougher to think about so maybe between now and the time it arrives we can think of a couple of good ones just in case.

I hope we don't have to use the boys names but I'd be happy with boys too I guess.

Darling I love you and I'm allright. Please forgive me for the short letters, but it can't be helped.

All my love for an eternity,

Jim (dada soon)

P.S. I LOVE YOU SWEETHEART.

Me

●●●

March 26, 1967: III MAF (Marine Amphibious Force) was ordered to prepare a plan for locating, constructing, and occupying a strongpoint obstacle system south of the DMZ to prevent the North Vietnamese from infiltrating through that zone into South Vietnam. What became known as "McNamara's Wall" began construction later in the year with strategic strong points forcing infiltrators into 'corridors' where they could be located and destroyed by American planes, artillery and infantry.

March 29, 1967

Dearest Darling,

I received your package today but I have no time to write a long letter. I just got in from a Long Range Patrol and its getting dark. I received letters from Jan, my mom & Grandma and Grandma in LZ, and Aunt Dolly. Please tell my mom I'll write as soon as I can. I'm allright and I love you very much. I'm just writing fast before it gets too dark.

Thank you so much for the package I really enjoyed the cookies. Honey the pictures are great. I hope they don't get ruined in the weather in this place. The guys think you are gorgeous. I told you so.

I love you so much and really miss you and need you more than anything.

All my love forever,
Jim

P.S. I LOVE YOU!
Me

March 29, 1967: search and destroy mission Operation Summerall began in the highlands of Darlac, Khanh Hoa and Phu Yen Provinces, between Buon Ea Yang and Khanh Duong.

March 30, 1967

My Darling Wife,

Right now I should have plenty of time to write you a letter instead of a note. I'm sorry that yesterdays letter was so short but I didn't have time to breathe. They had me doing one thing after another.

I don't have any of your letters with me right now so I can't answer very well.

I was on Long Range Patrol for the last 3 days and didn't have a chance to write anybody. I received your package yesterday with all the goodies in it. Thank you so much.

Honey I know it will probably be more expensive but could you send me small cans of fruit, like fruit cocktail, peaches, pears, apricots, etc. I sure would like some.

Honey I might have to send those pictures back because I'm afraid they might get ruined. I cherish them dearly but I'm so afraid of getting them soiled.

Oh yeah! My hair is getting longer by the day. I just had a haircut today but it was just a trim. By the time I get my R&R I'll have the same old mop back.

This week our platoon has been building a new landing zone for helicopters. I hope we stay here for awhile, but I doubt it.

When we go back to An Khe (I hope in early June) we will definitely be guarding the Green Line which is really easy and safe. I'm looking forward to that but not as much as R&R in Hawaii with my loving wife.

...I'm really getting excited now about starting a family. The more I think about it the happier I am.

Do you realize how hard its going to be to leave you after my R&R and come back to this place. The only thing that will make it worthwhile is knowing that you may have a big surprise for me when I get back home.

Did I tell you that I started to grow a moustache? But I had to shave it off. Just because our 1st sergeant made up some rule about our company always being neat no matter where we are.

I didn't mind shaving it off because it made me look like a Hell's Angel or something. I was really grubby looking.

Our company used to be able to wear beards but they changed all that now.

There is still some talk about getting out of Vietnam earlier than one year.

This is what happened before.

The 1st cav all got out early last year around June, July and August. Now the 25th Infantry Division gets out early in Sept, October + November. I hope that the 1st cav gets out Dec. Jan +Feb next year because I might be home for Christmas. That is the way it works. One unit gets it at a time. So I hope you understand how it works and that you will keep your fingers crossed for me.

Darling I love you so much that I ache with passion. I want you to know that feeling of love I have for you but how can I in a letter?

Its so hard to write about and I really don't feel like its doing much good. But I know you understand as I do when you write.

Honey my sergeant just came by and told me he heard a rumor that we might be going to An Khe next month. I sure hope its not just a rumor. Its supposed to be around the 15th of April.

Honey I have to write some other letters but I will write again as soon as I can.

My everlasting love,

Jim

P.S. Much kisses and a big hug.

Love,

Jim

The month of March 1967 saw the second highest level of imports into North Vietnam of bulk petroleum and bulk food from Soviet ships. March was the third successive month in which China has shipped petroleum to North Vietnam on British flag ships / Free World ships.

Chapter Eight

APRIL 1967

"I thank God each night for my wife and my life and also enjoy every breath that I take and praise every morning I wake up to. It means another day gone, another day I'm alive, and another day closer to being home with my wife forever."

April 1, 1967

Hi Honey,

Guess what day this is? You can bet that I'm not going to tell you any April Fools Jokes. I feel like this place isn't worthy of American Traditions and customs.

...No darling I haven't changed at all. I thought I was but I guess it was my imagination. The only thing that has changed on me is my tan and a few scratches on my hands from thorn bushes.

Honey can you ever forgive me for not writing more often? I have been trying awfully hard to write to you but I just can't seem to get enough time to write. You should have received two letters together. That's a short one and a six page letter. On the short one I didn't have hardly any time to write.

Boy it sure is hot here! We've been working on this landing zone all week and it really gets hot on this hill.

Tomorrow or the next day we will be going back down the hill in to the valley again. I don't like it down there, but theres nothing I can do about it.

Well honey I've got to go right now so I better close and continue when I get back.

I'm back again. I was on another patrol and we had to search a village at the base of the hill. I just got back and I'm wringing wet from climbing up and down the hill.

Darling I know that when I finally get away from here we are going to be the happiest married couple in the world. I also hope to be very happy parents around June or July. I hope it can be July for 2 reasons.

One is that I don't want our child born too close too our anniversary and I would like Dennis to have the thrill of guessing whether or not it will be close to his birthday.

That will be something for Dennis to look forward to because he always seems to be left out of everything ever since he was a baby. I hope you don't mind. Try to think of a good date that suits you anyway because I really don't mind at all when it arrives.

I miss you so very much and need you more than ever. Please don't ever leave me. I know you won't but I like to hear you say it.

I give my heart bursting with love,
Jim

P.S. I love you.
Me

March 31- April 1, 1967: Battle of Ap Gu/LZ George VC assault and the fire fight lasted two days. 1st Infantry Division Arty fired over 15,000 rounds and 133 airstrikes were delivered.

April 2, 1967

Hi Sweetheart,

I received another letter from you last night and I sure am glad to know that you are my wife and are waiting for me to come home to give you my love in exchange for yours.

Guess what? We will be on this hill for 2 or 3 more days then we go back to Ahn Lo Valley. When we leave here we are going to have a tank attached to our outfit. That sure will help us a lot and prevent a lot of guys from getting wounded. I hope it stays with us the rest of the time we are in the field.

If it does a good job then we will get 5 more tanks. 3 of them will have 2 50 caliber machine guns plus a 105 Howitzer mounted on them. 2 others will have 1 50 caliber and one M-60 machine gun and 90 mm guns mounted on them and the last one will have 2 M60 machine guns and a flame thrower. If we get them all my job will consist of going around and counting dead VC.

It might be an unpleasant job but at least it will be a lot safer.

...I'm sure glad we got married when we did. Even though we have had it pretty rough during these past few months we still haven't given up on our plans for the future. Those plans and you my love are the only reasons for me to make it back alive and well.

I hope that if we have any sons that they don't have to go through what I am. Right from the beginning they are either going to join one of the services or go into a reserve unit. My sons will never be drafted and have to fight a war like this one.

Say, how are you doing with your hula lessons? Are you graceful yet or are you still trying to get the hang of it?

Honey, you just don't know how thankful I am that I have such a wonderful wife. I'm glad that you try to keep busy and make the time go fast for you. Those hula lessons were the best thing you could have done. I'm also happy that you are taking care of the bills as well. If I was married to someone else I'd probably be bankrupt by now. Honey I know its hard on you and believe me I appreciate everything you do for us. I don't think it will have to be like this all the time.

At least I can say that I truly have a loving and devoted wife when most men consider their wives a problem. The only problem I have with you is that we are too far apart. And that's not your fault anyway.

I've decided that October is the best time to take my R&R so I'll have the best chance to go to Hawaii. I'm going to talk to my sergeant about it later this month and sign up for it. Its only 6 months away and I think it would be better for both of us. I think the 1st of October would be better for starting a family too.

I <u>really</u> want to start a family now. Sometimes I stop whatever I am doing and think about it.

Honey theres not much more I can tell you today except that I love you very much and continually miss you. Say hello to your mom and dad and Mikie for me. I love you darling with all my heart.

Keep praying.

All my true love,

Jim

April 2, 1967: The 59-day rice protection and search & destroy operation in Phu Yen Province, Operation Adams, came to an end. Friendly losses were 46 killed and 278 wounded. Enemy losses were 491 killed and 33 detained.

April 3, 1967

Hi Honey,

Its April 3 and this makes the 4 letter in a row that I have written to you. I hope it makes up for all the lost time I had trying to write before.

Today I received the package you sent with the tablets, envelopes, cigarettes, soap and toothpaste.

Honey I really appreciate these things you are sending me but please hold off on the soap and toothpaste. I don't want to sound like a filthy kid but I only get to wash up or shave every 5 days or so and right now I'm just finishing the second bar of soap that I took from home. I've got toothpaste to last me for awhile also.

I have been trying my hardest to keep this letter from getting dirty but I guess its impossible when you are in the field.

Boy its so hot here right now I could drink a whole case of beer by myself but they don't give any beer when we're out in the field. The only time we get it is when we go to An Khe. I think that is a good policy anyway. Over here, beer is about like an ice cold coke would be at home, everyone drinks beer to cool off. It's a lot cheaper over here too unless you go into town. They charge 15¢ a can at the service club and in town its 80¢ a can.

These people are real crooks and they try to take G.I.'s for every cent they own. But they aren't going to get my money unless I feel the price is right.

I'm pretty sure that we will be going back to An Khe on the 15th of this month unless something changes the plans again. I'll be able to go into town and get another comfort set for you and maybe a jewelry box if I can find one.

This is April so please let me know as soon as you get that extra money I told you about and tell me how much it is. I don't even know how much money I'm making over here. Also let me know if you received another savings bond. If you haven't I can get it straightened out when I go to An Khe this month.

Honey I really, really, really, truly want a family. And I want it soon! The sooner we start the better I like the idea. I just pray that it takes effect on my R&R.

Darling I'll close now sending in every word of this letter all my love and deep devotion.

Se la amor

Forever,

Jim

P.S. It means "That's love" forever.

Your lovin' hubby,

Me

P.P.S. Thank you again sweetie for the package.

Me

Letters soiled with mud and water.

Every letter carried an endearment to Micki, most carried the inscription, "Aloha nui loa." Meaning, 'I love you' in Hawaiian.

April 3, 1967:

➤ *Operation Portsea commenced. The 12 day operation was designed to disrupt VC supply lines between Binh Gia and Xuyen Moc in Phuoc Tuy Province.*

➤ *In an address by Johnson to the Joint Session of the Tennessee State Legislation he stated, "Viet-Nam is aggression in a new guise, as far removed from the trench warfare as the rifle from the longbow. This is a war of infiltration, of subversion, of ambush."*

April 4, 1967

Dearest Darling,

Today is a day that I can feel nothing else to talk about except our love.

Sweetheart, I know we were made for each other, just as the moon was made for the sky.

Without the moon to light the sky at night, there would be nothing but dark, lonely emptiness. And just as you were meant for me and I for you, without your love to brighten my life, I too would be wandering about in a sea of darkness. I would never have the opportunity to see the light of love and true devotion if it were not for you my darling.

During the short time we have actually been man and wife to each other, I have felt so much of love and the wonderful feeling you get when it is shared equally.

Our lives now face the strange and new excitement of a new member to our lives. A small joy of having this wonderful miracle happen to us would be the ultimate possession of the love that binds forever our lives.

Darling do you realize the wonderful experience that we are about to encounter? Having a baby join in on the love we have for each other and the love and attention that we both can generate into caring for our child could only be gifted to those who deserve the happiness that only God himself can give.

To believe in the feeling of true love is the most time consuming and most rewarding to anyone such as we have experienced.

How was that for a love letter?

...Every once in awhile I get a very strong urge to write words of love to my one and only love.

I must close now because it is getting dark. I will write again soon.

> My love is all for you.
>> Jim

I love you Mrs. Piper.

Till death do us part in about 100 years.   Your hubby.

April 4, 1967:

> ➢ *Martin Luther King delivered his "Beyond Vietnam" speech at Riverside Church condemning the Vietnam War. Declaring, "my conscience leaves me no other choice," King described the war's deleterious effects on both America's poor and Vietnamese peasants, and insisted that it was morally imperative for the U.S. to take radical steps to halt the war through nonviolent means.*

> ➢ *Hanoi would not permit more newsmen to visit North Vietnam because there was debate within North Vietnam about the value of New York Times editor Harrison Salisbury's visit to, and subsequent reporting on, North Vietnam.*

April 5, 1967: Operation Francis Marion commenced guarding operations along the Cambodian border in Pleiku Province against the NVA. Multiple brigades and divisions supported this operation until its cessation on October 12, 1967.

April 6, 1967

Hi Darling,

Did you enjoy that last letter? I wrote it on the spur-of-the-moment. Every once in awhile I get the urge to write like that. Tell me if you would like some more letters like the last one.

...Right now we are at the northern tip of the Ahn Lo Valley at the base of the mountains.

Tomorrow we will rendezvous with a whole tank brigade and make a sweep south in a final effort to get Charlie out of the valley.

Right now he is completely surrounded and we have 3 brigades plus a tank brigade here to wipe him out.

That's approximately 35,000 G.I.'s and about 400 tanks plus their crews.

There is only 4 battalions of Charlies in the valley (about 8,000) so that makes the odds in our favor about 5 ½ to 1. Now the only problem we have is finding the little bastard.

If this last push south is a success I'll be spending most of my time at L.Z. English training South Vietnamese Troops so they can keep the VC from re-entering the valley.

Sounds great doesn't it. Well its not going to be as easy as said. Charlie knows how and where to hide so we can't detect him. I just hope those tanks scare the hell out of him to make him either surrender or start running from his hiding place.

You are going to think I'm real mean but I had to slap an old woman across the face to make her talk yesterday.

She had a picture of her son and I asked her if he was viet cong. All we have to say to her is "Um son Viet Cong?" She shook her head and started crying. Then the interpreter came over and asked where he was and she wouldn't tell him so I was instructed to slap her every time she wouldn't answer.

I felt bad, just as if I had slapped Grandma Pacheco. But afterwards I found out that I should have beat her to death because she had a hand grenade on a chain around her neck and it was hanging between her boobs so it couldn't be seen. If she would have pulled the pin we all would have been picking fragments out of our butts.

There is still some talk about us going back to An Khe on the 15th of April but its still not for sure yet. I'll let you know as soon as I get the final word.

...I'm going to have to close this letter pretty quick because I am going out on an ambush patrol. I've been on two of them already and haven't seen any Charlies yet but this one is supposed to bring some results. I like ambushes because Charlie gets all shook up and don't know where we are or where the firing is coming from.

Most of the time he gets wiped out completely and we don't suffer any casualties. I wish ambushes were all we did.

Time to go now so take care and I'll be seeing you soon.

Love and radiance to us forever,
Jim

April 6, 1967: Quang Tri City was attacked by 2500 Viet Cong and NVA. The Quang Tri Province jail was also attacked and 220 prisoners were released (enemy guerillas and cadres). Friendly losses were 99 killed, 138 wounded. Enemy losses were 77.

April 7, 1967 Operation Lejuene began.

The 1st Cavalry Division was given less than twelve hours to put a battalion task force into the Duc Pho area and less than 36 hours to increase that force to brigade size. The principal reason behind this operation was an urgent Marine requirement to free some of their troops in Quang Ngai for movement further north. In deference to the Marines, the operation was named after Major General John Archer Lejeune, a Marine leader during the Spanish American War and World War I.

The boundary between the provinces of Quang Ngai to the north and Binh Dinh to the south established the demarcation line between the I Corps and II Corps Tactical Zones. This same boundary line divided the U. S. military effort, with the III Marine Amphibious Force having the responsibility in the I Corps area.

Throughout its previous nineteen months of operations in Vietnam, the 1st Cavalry had never operated outside of the II Corps area and no U.S. Army combat unit had operated in the I Corps Tactical Zone. The enemy assumed that they would be secure by moving into the "safe" area of Quang Ngai Province and elude the pursuit by the 1st Cavalry Division. This proved to be a poor assumption.

In his last letter dated April 9, 1967, Jim Piper wrote:

My darling wife,

Honey, IF anything should happen to me, you will be notified by the American Red Cross.

Darling, you are next of kin now and always will be. Now in the event that I should get lightly wounded, I will notify you myself. But if I get seriously wounded or get killed (heaven forbid) you will be notified first, not my parents.

...I can imagine the two of us in Hawaii and I keep wishing the time will go by faster so I could be there sooner with you.

...Darling I'm so sorry I had to burn that big card you sent me. It was such a wonderful card that I showed it to everybody. But not the letter. I had to get rid of it because we were not going to come back to An Khe for quite awhile and the card would have gotten ruined anyway.

Darling I don't mind you showing people my letters but please don't show them the letters that are meant just for you like that last mushy one I wrote you.

As soon as I get discharged I'm going to go to General Foods and tell them I want a couple weeks to get reorganized and then I'll start. They won't mind a couple more weeks if they have waited two years. Besides I will want to spend a little time with my wife. Especially if we have a child or 2 to take care of. I'll have to get to know my child too.

...Honey don't worry about my R&R in October because no matter where I am I will go. Even if I'm in the field during the middle of a big battle I'll go when my R&R says so. Just before the last fire fight a guy went on R&R and didn't have to fight. He was pulled out one 1 hour before we made the air assault.

Well, we only have 3 more days to go before we go to An Khe. Boy am I glad. But Lord knows where I'll go after that. Now don't get scared but there has been some talk about the brigade moving to the DMZ in June. But I don't think I will have to go because I'm in the 1st Brigade that I think we will be guarding the bridge on Highway 19.

When I get stationed stateside I'll be able to live off post with my wife no matter what rank I am. I hope I'll be a sergeant when I get back. If not I'll be happy just to _be_ back. Even so you can live with me when I get home.

The weather is still pretty hot with occasional showers but not heavy rain.

Honey I sure appreciate those long letters but by the time I finish reading them I hardly have time to write.

I had better close now and write to mom...Just remember that you are the only one that gets all my love at the end of the letter and only you get "Aloha nui loa" on the envelope.

I thank God each night for my wife and my life and also enjoy every breath that I take and praise every morning I wake up to. It means another day gone, another day I'm alive, and another day closer to being home with my wife forever.

Every once of love to you sweetie.

Jim

"I thank God each night for my wife and my life and also enjoy every breath I take and praise every moring I wake up to. It means another day gone, another day I'm alive, and another day closer to being home with my wife forever.
Every once of love to you sweetie
Jim"

James Dennis Piper was killed in action April 11, 1967, two days after writing his last letter.

According to the telegram from the Secretary of the Army received on April 13, 1967, Jim was killed on a combat operation when hit by hostile fire.

Jim would have turned 20 years old April 20, 1967.

WFRC49 SPF036 LD027 SYA034 SY WA096 XV GOVT PD   1967 APR 13 AM 7 47

FAX WASHINGTON DC 13 312A EST

MR AND MRS CLENETH L PIPER, DONT PHONE DONT DLR BTWN 10PM AND

6AM

16192 CHANNEL ST SAN LORENZO CALIF

THE SECRETARY OF THE ARMY HAS ASKED ME TO EXPRESS HIS DEEP REGRET

THAT YOUR SON, PRIVATE FIRST CLASS JAMES D. PIPER DIED IN VIETNAM

ON 11 APRIL 1967. HE WAS ON A COMBAT OPERATION WHEN HIT BY HOSTILE

SMALL ARMS FIRE.

PLEASE ACCEPT MY DEEPEST SYMPATHY. YOUR DAUGHTER-IN-LAW

WILL FURNISH INSTRUCTIONS FOR THE RETURN OF YOUR LATE SON

KENNETH G WICKHAM MAJOR GENERAL, USA F-3 THE ADJUTANT GENERAL

(42).

624A PST APR 13 67

COMPANY "A"
1ST BATTALION (AIRBORNE) 8TH CAVALRY
1ST CAVALRY DIVISION (AIRMOBILE)
APO SAN FRANCISCO, CALIFORNIA 96490

Mr. & Mrs. Clemeth L. Piper   7 MAY 1967
16192 Channel Street
San Lorenzo, California
93304

Dear Mr. and Mrs. Piper

    I extend my most profound sympathy to you on the loss of your
son, Private First Class James D. Piper, who died in the service of
his country on 11 April 1967.

    On the afternoon of 11 April 1967, our company was on a search
and destroy mission in Binh Dinh Province, Republic of Vietnam.
James served as a rifleman in the second platoon. As we crossed a
flat, grassy marsh area, your son was struck by small weapons fire.
It may be of some comfort to know that James died instantly and was
not subject to suffering.

    Your son had been in Company A for only a short time, but had
already began to establish himself as one of the finest young soldiers in the unit. His enthusiasm and devotion to duty was a spark
that ignited all of those around him. He displayed the finest soldi-
erly bearing, discipline and conduct. I am proud to have served with
him. Your son was greatly respected by all those who knew him and
will truly be missed. Upon the return of the battalion to base camp,
a memorial service will be held in the battalion chapel.

    Your son's personal effects have been gathered and sent home.

    On behalf of the officers and men of my command, I extend my per-
sonal sympathy and pray the Lord will be with you in this time of
sorrow.

                                        With deepest sympathy,

                                        JEROME A. DIEBOLD
                                        Captain, Infantry
                                        Commanding

The U.S. expenditure in Vietnam for the fiscal year 1967 was $21 billion.

At the end of 1967 there were an estimated 486,000 US troops in Vietnam.

Total US soldiers KIA in Vietnam 1967: 11,153.

By the end of the war the total numbers estimated to be: KIA 58,267, WIA 303,644, MIA 1,711, with a total of nearly 3.5 million that served in the Vietnam theater of operations.

Micki's memories

The first time Micki laid eyes on Jim she was smitten.

Attending a dinner/dance with her Aunt at the Oakland Hawaiian Club, Hui Kamaina (come a i na), Micki spotted Jim across the room. He was playing the drums in a band, The Galaxies, with his brother Gary as lead singer and guitarist. "I can't remember who made the first move, but I'm sure it was me. We were together until the day he died; no one else."

Jim attended San Lorenzo High School in San Lorenzo while Micki attended Sunset High School in Hayward.

Dating throughout high school, Jim and Micki attended each other's formal dances and shared a love of music. A year after they graduated high school, and gainfully employed the two became one on June 18, 1966. Soon after, Jim received his draft notice. "It was a shock. The month flew by so quickly, there was not a day we were not together and surrounded by friends and family. It was the fastest month of our lives."

After Jim reported to the Armed Forces Induction Station in Oakland, California on August 30, 1966 Micki moved back home to be with her mother, father and little brother, to not only save money but so "that I wouldn't be alone."

Though Micki worked every day she remembers waiting each day for the mail to come, in hopes of receiving a letter. "I could almost hear his voice when I read the letters. It never occurred to me that he needed my letters as badly as I needed his. I literally lived from letter to letter, and now that I look back, I know that he too lived from letter to letter, desperately."

Micki was informed of her husband Jim Piper's death on April 13, 1967.

The memory of that day has been etched into Micki's mind forever, not seeming to diminish with the passage of time.

44 years later Micki relived that day…

"I was sitting in the living room with my younger brother Michael (Mikey), my mom and dad had gone to a little league meeting but for some reason my mom had left the phone number of the home they would be at for the meeting. I asked her why she would leave the number, she never had before, she just shrugged and gave me the number and said, 'just in case.'

My brother and I sat down in front of the tv to write letters to Jim. Not soon after my mother left, a nice looking soldier in a dress uniform came to the front door. I thought for sure Jim was playing a prank on me sending one of his friends to my mother's house; he would do that, when he knew someone that lived nearby was coming home on leave he would get them to stop by and check on me, I opened it expecting to receive a message from Jim. It was then that the soldier asked if I was Mrs. Piper. When I looked dumb struck, he clarified, 'Mrs. James Dennis Piper?' I knew right then that Jim was gone.

I still remember to this day the pain, the sobbing and the soldier trying to console me. I somehow called my mother, only remembering that I said 'Jim was killed.' She seemed to appear by my side, just like that.

I had to call Jim's parents. All I could say was 'Jim was killed.'

The Army was really good about staying by my side and bolstering me when I thought I could take no more. I remember looking at Jim's glass covered coffin, and then nothing. I went down. The man that was there to support me helped me up and whispered in my ear, 'Jim would want you to be strong.'

While women relatives wailed and scratched at the coffin crying for Jim to come back I noticed numbly that the memorial chapel was front to back, floor to ceiling flowers. The scent was overpowering. Almost sickening. To this day I will not buy flowers for a gravesite. I can't.

The procession for Jim was at least 100 cars long. I remember the soldier that was at the gates of the cemetery thought it was a dignitary being laid to rest.

My Jim lay just a few feet from Admiral Nimitz."

Reliving this part of her life has been an emotional drain but one that she feels is important to share, to make sure that people understand the soldier's point of view, not what Hollywood or the media portrays, but the human aspect and the fact that those boys and men that fought in Vietnam were brothers, fathers, sons, and husbands, and worthy of our respect, honor and recognition.

Micki has gone on with her life and in an ironic twist is happily married to a Vietnam Veteran.

"Though Jim was my first love, one I will never forget, I have had the good fortune of getting a second chance at true love. I have been married to my husband Larry Phillips for 23 years now and going strong. Larry has been supportive and encouraging while Charity and I worked on this project. I know at times it stirred up old emotions that I would have to deal with, but Larry was always there by my side, his love for me strong and unbending."

PRIVATE FIRST CLASS JAMES D. PIPER
KIA 11 April 67 in Vietnam
Presentation to Wife

By direction of the President, the Purple Heart is awarded posthumously

to ___Private First Class___ for wounds received in military operations
___James D. Piper___

in ___Vietnam___, against hostile foreign forces, which resulted in his

death on ___April 11th___.

This award, first established by General George Washington in 1782, is

presented to you as a tangible expression of your nation's gratitude and

everlasting appreciation for your ___husband's___ gallantry and devotion in

the service of his country

___James___ stands in the unbroken line of patriots who have

given their lives that our nation's goal of freedom and peace may be maintained.

I hope that this award and the knowledge of your ___husband's___ invaluable

contributions will serve to comfort you in the days that lie ahead.

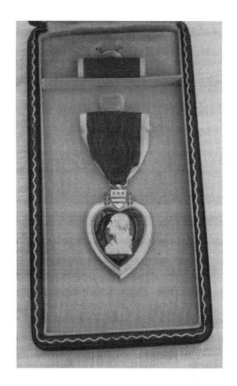

James Piper's Purple Heart, awarded posthumously.

The Purple Heart is a United States military decoration awarded in the name of the President to those who have been wounded or killed while serving on or after April 5, 1917 with the U.S. military.

Co A 1st Bn 8th Cav
1st Cav Div Airmobile

KIA April 11, 1967

PFC Kenneth Maurice Burnett, Winston Salem, NC
SSGT Bobby Walter Coleman, Houston, TX
PSGT Grant Madison Gilbreath, Monroe, MI
PFC Audeliz Hernandez-Pena, Perth Amboy, NJ
PFC Willis White Williams, Savannah, GA
PFC James Dennis Piper, San Lorenzo, CA

1ˢᵗ Cavalry

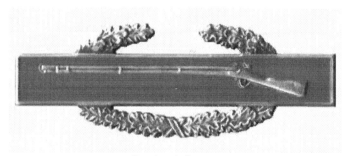

Combat Infantry

The Combat Infantryman Badge (CIB) is the U.S. Army combat service recognition decoration awarded to soldiers—enlisted men and officers (commissioned and warrant) holding colonel rank or below, who *personally* fought in active ground combat while an assigned member of either an infantry or a Special Forces unit, of brigade size or smaller, any time after 6 December 1941.

(8ᵗʰ Cavalry Regiment was first organized September 21, 1866 Angel Island, California)

Vietnam Service

Vietnam Campaign   National Defense

(L) Vietnam Military Merit Medal Awarded by the Republic of Vietnam, the Vietnamese equivalent to the United States Medal of Honor and was authorized to those soldiers who had performed extreme acts of bravery or had given their lives in armed combat with enemy forces of Vietnam.

(R) Republic of Vietnam Gallantry Cross Medal, awarded to any military personnel who have accomplished deeds of valor or displayed heroic conduct while fighting an enemy force.

Jim was the oldest of four boys.
Picture circa 1950's.
Left to right: Dennis, Jim, Tom, and Gary.

On April 11, 1967, Dennis was 16, Tom was 12 and Gary was 18 when Jim was killed in action at the age of 19, just 17 days shy of his 20th birthday.

Pictured, Jim's younger brothers Dennis and Tom, Memorial Day 2011.

Jim's brother Gary Piper 2011

The Brothers Remember

April 11, 1967:

Gary, Jim's younger brother by 14 months, was at his girlfriend's house when his dad called and told him that Jim had been hit. "I didn't know until I got home that he had been killed. My mother was out of control with grief and anger."

Dennis had been playing at a friend's house when his father came to collect him. Dennis remembers being upset because he was playing and he couldn't figure out why he had to come home so quickly. As his father walked him across the street he informed Dennis that Jim had been shot. "It wasn't until I was in the house and I saw my mother crying that my father told me Jim had died." In Dennis' memory, the days leading up to the funeral happened so quickly it was a blur, yet the funeral "is as clear as if it was today...the bad make-up, the stained collar..." not the way Dennis wanted to see his brother for the last time.

Tom remembers being upstairs doing homework when his father, in a strange voice, called for him to come down. "The next thing I remember was being at the funeral and the suffocating scent of flowers... I was young, but I can still remember the smell of those flowers." Though he valiantly clings to his last positive memory of his brother Jim when he left him at the Oakland base, "I remember the last time I saw him, I gave him a big hug."

Gary served in the Air National Guard from '65 – '71. "Jim's and my friends were mostly the same, we were so close in age, most of our friends were either getting drafted or joining up. By the end of my senior year most of my friends had already gone, I joined that summer."

Dennis tried to enlist just days after Jim was killed. Walking into the recruiter's office he told them he wanted to go to Nam, when asked why, his response was simple, "To kill the mother f___s that killed my brother." He was not allowed to enlist.

Tom also tried to enlist when he became of age, but his mother was too weak to handle the potential fallout of that decision. The thought of possibly losing another son to that war was too much for her to bear. He did not finish the testing process.

Gary is reminded of Jim every time he hears of a soldier losing his life in the Middle East, Christmas, Jim's birthday and at family get- togethers. "And sometimes there doesn't seem to be a trigger...he just comes to me."

Both Dennis and Tom, to this day, are greatly affected by the pungent scent of floral arrangements and avoid flower shops and floral departments in markets. Each has flashbacks when taps is played or guns are fired in succession. The flashback always takes them to the glass covered open coffin where they last saw their brother lay, paste white and lifeless.

We All Cry On Your Birthday
Music and lyrics by Gary Piper ©1980

The years don't seem so long
I remember like it was yesterday
Oh, brother, I wish I could know you
And look into your eyes today

I wonder what you'd be doin'
Where you'd live and would you have a family
And I wonder which way you'd be goin'
Would we be close; would we know each others' dreams

And We All Cry On Your Birthday
At Christmas and when old friends come around
And I remember the day when they took you away
And lowered you into the ground

As boys, life seemed a play thing
With never a thought it might end
But now the one thought each day brings
Is we don't know each other as men

And We All Cry On Your Birthday
At Christmas and when old friends come around
And I remember the day when they took you away
And lowered you into the ground

And Papa tried hard not to show it
But it's always so present in mom
The grief of losing her young son
In the jungles of Viet Nam

And We All Cry On Your Birthday
At Christmas and when old friends come around
And I remember the day when they took you away
And lowered you into the ground

Honorable Service

in the Armed Forces of the United States of America

In grateful Memory of

PRIVATE FIRST CLASS   JAMES DENNIS PIPER   US 56 822 929

Who Died while in the Service of our Country

as a Member of the

Army of the United States

on the 11TH *day of* APRIL 1967 *This certificate is awarded*

as a testimonial of Honest and Faithful Service

Stanley R. Resor
Secretary of the Army

DEPARTMENT OF THE ARMY
HEADQUARTERS, 1ST CAVALRY DIVISION (AIRMOBILE)
OFFICE OF THE COMMANDING GENERAL
IN REPLY REFER TO   APO SAN FRANCISCO 96490

26 APR 1967

Mr. & Mrs. Clemeth L. Piper
16192 Channel Street
San Lorenzo, California
94580

Dear Mr. & Mrs. Piper,

Please accept my most profound sympathy on the recent loss of your son, Private First Class James D. Piper, Company A, 1st Battalion, 9th Cavalry, who died in the service of his country on 11 April 1967.

James' death came as a shock to all who knew him. He was a dedicated American, who was well liked and respected by his fellow soldiers.

I sincerely hope that you will be comforted in your sorrow by the abiding faith we all share in our common Christian cause.

Sincerely,

JOHN J. TOLSON
Major General, USA
Commanding

Engraved brick donated by Micki & Larry Phillips in 2010,
permanently displayed in the 150th Anniversary Copperopolis
Commemorative Wall in honor of James Dennis Piper.

GLOSSARY

A.I.T. – Advanced Individual Training (Army)

ARVN – Army of the Republic of Vietnam

Bat – Battalion

Bivouac – a temporary encampment under little or no shelter

BLT – Battalion Landing Force

Boonies – colloquial shortening of boondocks c.1965, originally among U.S. troops in Vietnam War in reference to rural areas of the country as opposed to Saigon.

Cav – Cavalry

CIDG – Civilian Irregular Defense Group (a program that began in late 1961 as a counterinsurgency experiment in the central highlands of South Vietnam. Under the direction of the CIA.)

CINPAC – Commander in Chief Pacific Command

CJCS – Chairman Joint Chiefs of Staff

DCI – Director of Criminal Intelligence

Distinguished Service Medal – the highest non-valorous military and civilian decoration of the United States.

DMZ – Demilitarized Zone

GVN – Government of the Republic of Vietnam

JCS – Joint Chiefs of Staff

Johnson – President Lyndon Baines Johnson 1963- 1969

KIA – Killed in Action

LZ – Landing Zone

MACV – Military Assistance Command, Vietnam

MAF – Marine Amphibious Force

MIA – Missing in Action

Montagnard – Vietnamese indigenous tribesmen

NFLSV – National Front for the Liberation of South Vietnam

NVA – North Vietnamese Army

NVN – North Vietnam

P X- Post Exchange (a store operated by the Army and Air Force Exchange Service on US Army posts.)

PFC – Private First Class

PVT - Private

Peoples Republic of China – commonly known as China

ROK – Republic of Korea

SNAFU – Situation Normal All F----d Up

SLF – Special Landing Force

Tet – Vietnamese New Year

United Nations - an international organization whose stated aims are facilitating cooperation in international law, international security, economic development, social progress, human rights, and achievement of world peace.

USARV – US Army Vietnam

VC – Viet Cong

USIB – United States Intelligence Board

Viet Cong – (National Liberation Front) was a political organization and army in South Vietnam and Cambodia that fought the United States and South Vietnamese governments during the Vietnam War.

White Paper – an authoritative report or guide

WIA – Wounded in Action

All the letters in this book were written by James Dennis Piper and reprinted verbatim. When a sentence ends or begins with a series of dots this is where whole sentences were intentionally left out to due to the highly personal nature and/or were replies to questions asked in previous letters from Micki.

The following sites were used, with written permission or exist in the public domain, for research.

http://www.armchairgeneral.com

Lyndon Baines Johnson Library

www.slzvets.com

Gerald R. Ford Library

Pentagon Papers- Declassified per executive order 13526 Section 3.3 :
Part IV-C-6-a 'Evolution of the War' Direct Action: The Johnson Commitments, 1964-1968 U.S. Ground Strategy and Force Deployment

Part IV-C-6-b 'Evolution of the War' Direct Action: The Johnson Commitments, 1964-1968 U.S. Ground Strategy and Force Deployments 1965-1967

Part IV-C-6-c 'Evolution of the War' Direct Action: The Johnson Commitments 1964-1968 U.S. Ground Strategy and Force Deployments

Part IV-C-8 'Evolution of the War' – Direct Action: The Johnson Commitments 1964-1968 Re-emphasis on Pacification

Part V-A-Vol-IID 'Justification of the War' – The Johnson Administration

Charity L. Maness lives in the foothills of Northern California.

Charity's interest in supporting Veterans began when in an effort to better help her USMC son coming home from the Middle East transition, she began a movement to form a VFW Post in her small town. Through working with the many local veterans of foreign wars she developed a love of their stories, their courage and their devotion to country.

When the opportunity arose to honor one of their fallen, she welcomed it with open arms.

"I would like to take this opportunity to thank all veterans, from the bottom of my heart, for your service."

Forever in your debt,

Charity L. Maness

For more information about the author, visit her blog site at charitymaness.blogspot.com.

To email the author write to charitymaness@live.com.

Author photo by MD Portraits
Cover photo by Ric Ryan (USMC Vietnam '67- '68)

If you or someone you love needs Veteran assistance visit http://www.va.gov/ or call the VA talk line at 1-800-273-8255

Proof

Made in the USA
Charleston, SC
10 January 2012